HOW I TAUGHT MICHAEL SLATER TO PLAY CRICKET

HOW I TAUGHT MICHAEL SLATER TO PLAY CRICKET

WARREN SMITH WITH TERRY SMITH

ABC Books

Published by ABC Books for the
AUSTRALIAN BROADCASTING CORPORATION
GPO Box 9994 Sydney NSW 2001

First published October 2006

National Library of Australia
Cataloguing-in-Publication entry
Smith, Warren Harold, 1947- .
How I taught Michael Slater to play cricket.

Includes index.
ISBN 978 0 7333 1762 0.

ISBN 0 7333 1762 6.

1. Cricket - Coaching - Handbooks, manuals, etc. 2. Cricket - Australia. 3. Cricket players - Australia. I. Smith, Terry, 1937- . II. Slater, Michael, 1970- . III. Australian Broadcasting Corporation. IV. Title.

796.358077

Cover design by Blue Cork
Designed by Kerry Klinner, Mega City Design
Set in Sabon 10/14
Printed and bound by Griffin Press, Adelaide

5 4 3 2 1

CONTENTS

FOREWORD

MICHAEL SLATER

If there is one word to describe Warren Smith, it's passion. It simply oozes out of him. He has an absolute passion for cricket and what he believes in.

Warren is one of a kind. Something clicked the moment I saw him when I went to one of his Monday coaching classes at the Mt Austin Primary School in Wagga at the age of seven. Warren seemed to talk at a million words a minute and, as you might expect from a man with red hair, he stood no nonsense. He was a perfectionist — everything had to be done properly, and I responded to that.

Since that first day, Warren has been my personal coach and advisor. When my mother left the family when I was twelve, we were distraught. With Dad doing his damndest to keep things going, Warren was really fantastic, in some ways becoming a second father to me. I could have lost direction, but he kept me on track and has been a great sounding board ever since. A real stabiliser. Warren has never pushed himself but has always been there when I needed him.

Warren Smith with the poster saluting Michael Slater's first Test century
Courtesy the *Daily Advertiser*, Wagga Wagga

Whatever I might have achieved in cricket, I owe a large part of it to Warren Smith. Things stuck that I learned from him at a very early age. He believes in the basics of the game, in discipline and in hard work. There must be no cutting of corners.

He quickly got through to me that footwork is the key to batting, and I like to think that footwork and hand speed were the strengths of my play. It's the same with a boxer, and I'm not surprised Warren has struck up a friendship with the famous boxing trainer, Johnny Lewis.

I feel some coaches have become too dependent on their computers. There is certainly a place for technology in modern-day cricket, but you can't get away from hard work. You must get down and get dirty. That's what Warren Smith is: a get-down-and-get-dirty coach.

Warren is big on the little disciplines, the one percent things. As a kid I was delighted when I reached fifty for the first time, but although

Warren was happy, he pointed out it would have been even better if my shirt hadn't been hanging out. Hands in the pocket were another no-no. 'Get your hands out of your Davy Crocketts,' he'd say.

With all the razzamatazz of Twenty20 and one-day cricket, standards have slipped, and all the time you see guys with their shirts hanging out. I don't like it because it goes against the etiquette of the game I was taught by Warren.

He loves to break down an innings, saying it's about reaching little milestones like blocks of ten. You don't think about a hundred — rather, concentrate on getting to ten, then twenty and then thirty. I won't say I always stuck to this plan, but as usual he's on the money.

The day I scored my first Test hundred at Lord's, Warren was with me every step of the way, celebrating each ten runs with a beer as he watched on TV. The result was a very emotional phone call from Wagga that night as we relived the moment.

Because his batting drills are second to none, some people might think that Warren is basically a batting specialist, but his coaching is all-encompassing. When he offers an opinion on fielding and bowling, even the top players take heed.

Warren could well have climbed the coaching ladder to the very top if he'd moved to Sydney, but he's stayed a country boy who's been happy to do the bulk of his coaching in the bush. Still, he has achieved so much.

His life revolves around cricket, and more specifically around bringing on the kids. I'm delighted this remarkable man has chosen to share his unique coaching secrets.

Two good old boys from Wagga Wagga ... Warren Smith and Geoff Lawson

FOREWORD

GEOFF LAWSON

Without any fear of contradiction, I say that Warren Smith is the finest batting coach in Australia.

Along with innovative drills, he has this incredible knowledge that goes outside the orthodox coaching manual. Warren always is looking for an edge, and when he's got something to say he grabs your brain, and no matter whether you're a Test player or a junior cricketer, you listen.

Not only does Warren have lots of intriguing ideas, he also has the enthusiasm and people skills to get them across. When he found Michael Slater, it's no surprise he turned him into a Test player. With Warren it's all go, go, go, go — hence his three heart attacks. At matches he is like a cat on a hot tin roof. His jaws chomping on a piece of chewing gum, he walks around the ground tossing a ball from hand to hand.

I go back a long way with Warren Smith. He was a very good player when I was a teenager growing up in Wagga, and our paths crossed many times on the cricket field. We played rep matches together and perhaps he could have played State cricket if he'd stayed in Sydney for four or five years. We'll never know.

Warren loves seeing people do well, particularly young kids, and when he installed a bowling machine in the tyre business in the main street at Wagga where he worked, everyone was welcome to practise there in the winter months. I played for another club but that didn't matter at all. This man was born to coach.

I headed to Sydney and was starting to play Test cricket when I ran into Warren. 'Henry, I've got this young bloke called Michael Slater,' he said. 'He's pretty good.' Michael Slater? The last time I'd seen him he was a four-year-old annoying people at a junior cricket practice when I was coaching.

Warren understands first-class cricketers and it's a shame that so far he hasn't coached at a higher level. When Steve Rixon coached NSW, he brought in Warren to work with the batsmen. VVS Laxman sought him out for coaching when the Indian champion came to Sydney for treatment of an injury. When the University of NSW team made a trip to India in 2005, Warren, who was our club coach, was hailed as a hero because the cricket-crazy locals knew he was Michael Slater's coach.

Apart from personally coaching one of Australia's finest Test batsmen, Warren has taken Dominic Thornely to the verge of getting a game for Australia, developing the skills that have won him recognition as the finest fielder in the country.

Every player matters to Warren, whether they're a Test cricketer or a fifth grader. He wants all of them to succeed but demands they work hard practising their skills to the nth degree. It's not good enough just having a hit and wandering about doing a few throw-downs. There are no short cuts. Warren demands blood, sweat and tears, and if you're not doing the business, he'll let you know.

Warren Smith is a very practical coach who teaches practical skills. He's adamant the essence of successful batting is quick feet, and has developed drills to hone and improve this facet of the game. Drills that keep the players interested.

Some people are sceptical of Warren's methods because he's different. To them, he's an enigma because they don't understand what he's doing. I see him as a remarkable man who is years ahead of his time.

INTRODUCING WARREN SMITH

He is a tough old nugget, red haired and sunburnt with the salt of the Australian bush in him. Warren Smith comes from Wagga Wagga and learned his cricket on malthoid and concrete pitches where a piece of chalk is kept behind the middle stump so the batsman can mark centre on grounds surrounded by gaunt gums. It was there that a wiry seven year old called Michael Slater turned up for one of his schoolboy coaching classes.

Warren's passion for the game is unquenchable. He has shrugged off three heart attacks as if they were speed bumps, nervously tossing a ball from hand to hand as he watches his pupils in action. The chewing gum Warren has got through over the years would run into tonnes. He's instantly friendly and always pragmatic, a crafty old fox who demands his players work hard and get the basics right.

The essence of Warren's coaching is simplicity coupled with a knack for innovation. As he believes batting is all about footwork, he made several visits to the gym when world boxing champion Kostya Tszyu was training to study this aspect of his craft. He insists on having a bicycle and skipping rope in the dressing room, and his Wazza Catch, in which a tennis ball is attached to the wrist by a string of elastic, has proved an invaluable coaching aid.

One day Warren was coaching at the SCG nets when a slim, trim young Indian introduced himself and said, 'Mr Smith, you are the man who coached the great Michael Slater. I like what you have taught him.' His name was VVS Laxman, a batsman who was to take the heart out of the Australian bowlers over the years. He was here for treatment of an injury, and after watching Warren go through his unique drills, Laxman asked if he too could work with him. Warren gave the Indian a copy of some illustrated sheets entitled 'The Slater Drills' and agreed to Laxman's request for a coaching lesson. When they crossed paths at a Prime Minister's XI game in Canberra several years later, Laxman said, 'Mr Smith, I still carry your drills in my cricket bag.'

FINDING A STAR

But let's begin at the beginning. Warren Smith was born in the NSW country town of West Wyalong on 10 November 1947 and when he was nine the family moved to Wagga Wagga, where his father John managed a sawmill. With the magnificent Murrumbidgee River flowing through it, Wagga, which gets its name from an Aboriginal word meaning 'many crows', is a vibrant city of 57,000 people and is the hub of the Riverina.

With the family short of money when his dad became ill with heart problems, Warren left school at fourteen to take a job in the sports section at David Jones, run by Ken McMullen, a former Wallaby rugby halfback who'd been a team-mate of Doug Walters in the NSW 2nd XI. Warren had played first grade for Wagga Wagga Cricket Club at the age of thirteen, and four years later he caught the train to Sydney to try his luck in first grade for Sutherland at the urging of former Test batsman Norm O'Neill, who'd seen him bat in a country trial.

In his first game he was the victim of a bombardment from Test fast bowler Frank Misson, who fired blistering bouncers around his ears before he was run out. In the next match against Bankstown, Warren was run out for a second time, and when his ailing father died in his arms a few weeks later he decided to stay home in Wagga rather than make the train trip to Sydney each Saturday.

By this stage Warren had made up his mind that he wanted to be a coach, but everybody laughed at him. Fearful for his future, his mother

The smile of a crafty old fox

Mary, with whom he had a wonderful rapport, demanded to know if it would pay the bills.

Soon he was running Monday-night coaching clinics at Mt Austin Primary School, where one of his pupils was a blond-haired boy named Peter Sterling, who was to win fame in rugby league. Another was Julian Slater, who one day brought along his seven-year-old brother Michael. 'He's very, very keen,' said their dad Peter. 'Would you have a look at him?' Smith usually didn't take pupils until they were nine or ten, but there was something about this one as he hit balls from a tee with thirty other boys. Warren recalls: 'I took Michael to one side and threw a ball at him. He went whack, hitting an on-drive like Greg Chappell did, very upright, very correct with his elbow cocked. Jeez, I couldn't believe it, not at seven years. I'd never seen anything like it. I'm a great believer in skills and vision and balance and this kid had the lot.'

'You really do like cricket, don't you son,' asked the coach. 'Yes, Mr Smith,' said young Michael. 'Well, would you like me to coach you?' asked Warren. 'Yes, I'd like you to,' was the reply.

Warren went home very excited and told his wife Pam, a charming lass from the small town of Lockhart whom he met at the Wagga Leagues Club, that he'd found someone special. From that day he would drive his star pupil home at seven o'clock after training in his beaten-up blue ute. Their friendship blossomed. At twelve, Michael was in the NSW Primary Schools team, and he made it at hockey, too. Warren is adamant that he could have played for Australia at hockey, as well as having all the attributes of a champion boxer with his fast hands and nimble footwork.

In those early days, Michael was a perfectionist who would hit hundreds and hundreds of balls until he got it right. 'My arm was absolutely rooted from throwing balls so I bought a bowling machine,' said Warren. At that stage he was working at the long-gone Jubilee Tyre Service fitting tyres during the day and coaching in the evening. The bowling machine was set up in the back of the garage and, although he was playing for South Wagga, Warren allowed players from other clubs to use it for free.

The upward curve of Slater's career continued with selection in the various State age groups, and he came to Sydney to become leading run-scorer in the AW Green Shield competition with the Balmain club. However, Warren's relationship with the youngster had to survive a controversial ruling that could well have led to a parting of the ways. With the Wagga RSL team due to play in a grand final, he stunned the locals by dropping Michael from the side. Warren recalls: 'It was the hardest thing I've had to do in my whole career. I'll never forget it. Michael was only fourteen and opening the batting, that's how good he was, but the game before the final I saw him flinch. So I dropped him. I was only trying to protect him, but Michael broke down and wept and everybody hated me. They said I was finished with him.'

Four or five months later, Warren's phone rang. It was Michael. 'You were definitely right,' he said. 'I'll be staying.' The following season Wagga RSL again was in the grand final and Michael opened the batting, smashing the bowling to score 120.

Warren was a great admirer of the hands, footwork and quickness of Mark Ella, the Wallaby rugby hero, and saw Slater possessing similar attributes. 'If you haven't got nice hands, you'll never do any good in cricket,' he says. So Warren developed Michael's game of playing 'through the V' in the style of Greg Chappell. Playing with a free spirit, Slater progressed to the Australian Under 19s, clinching an invitation to attend the Australian Cricket Academy in Adelaide in 1989/90 with an innings of 198 against New Zealand in which he carved future Test bowler Chris Cairns to all parts of the ground. Feeling he could do no more for his young protégé, Warren realised Michael had to go to Sydney if he was to fulfil his potential.

He phoned Geoff Lawson, who himself had to leave Wagga to give himself a chance of becoming a Test quick bowler, and said, 'Look after this kid. He's as good as I've ever seen.' Soon Slater was playing for Lawson's club, the University of NSW. At twenty, he won a NSW cap and, after scoring 1005 runs in the old Sheffield Shield the following season, he was chosen for the 1993 Ashes tour of England and hammered the bowlers to hit up 152 in the second Test at Lord's. He celebrated reaching the century by punching the air and planting a big kiss on the Australian badge on his helmet.

Warren listened on the radio to every ball of that innings, celebrating with a drink or two as Michael reached various targets. They spoke that night, with tears being shed at each end of the phone. 'I was as p....d as ten Dean Martins,' Warren recalls, and the upshot was that he made his first overseas plane flight to watch Slater hit up 40 and 26 in the next Test at Trent Bridge from a viewing area reserved for players' friends and wives.

With his profile soaring, friends and admirers urged Warren to head to Sydney where he could become rich and famous, but he was happy to stay in Wagga and search for another Michael Slater like a prospector seeking a second golden nugget. 'I'm a country boy at heart,' he explains. 'You can smell the gum leaves.' Soon Warren unearthed a budding champion named Dominic Thornely, who went to Pakistan in 2005 with the Australia A team. A baggy green cap surely awaits him.

Michael Slater has referred to Warren many times as his second father, and Warren regards him as part of the family. 'Slater could win a Test match in the first session,' says his admiring mentor. 'With his passion for attacking play, he put bums on seats and when he was doing well, he always had a beautiful smile on his face. I've been at games where he got out and people left the ground.' Michael's many triumphs included fourteen Test hundreds and twenty-one fifties in seventy-four Tests, but sometimes he lost his way when approaching the century, being dismissed no fewer than nine times in the nineties.

A LIFE IN COACHING

When Warren Smith became captain-coach of the Wagga Wagga club when hardly out of his teens, the locals didn't know what hit them. Once-a-week training was increased to two afternoons, and players had to turn up an hour before the 1.30 pm start on match day. If a specialist batsman was bowled at practice, he had to run a lap of the ground with his pads on. Players were fined for bowling no-balls in matches and he made a slip cradle and used a tennis racket and tennis ball to sharpen other skills.

Warren has never been frightened to step outside the square to pluck ideas from other sports, including gridiron and softball. He got some clues from famed rugby league coach Jack Gibson over a beer at the Captain Cook Hotel near the Sydney Cricket Ground. Keep it simple, said Gibson. Let the blokes know what's happening, stick to fundamentals and don't inhibit natural flair. Smith has chatted with AFL legend Ron Barassi and drawn on the wisdom of boxing trainer Johnny Lewis.

From the days he worked as the repair man stringing rackets, sewing pads and fixing bats at David Jones, Warren has had a fascination with inventing new gear. Once he ripped an old cricket ball apart, took out the hard core of cork, synthetic rubber and fibre, replaced it with a tennis ball and sewed it up with a saddler's needle and waxed thread. Just perfect for the kids he was coaching. It looked like a real cricket ball but was much softer. Now he makes more than a thousand a year, either selling them or giving them away to other coaches. Like the old lady in the French Revolution who used to sit below the guillotine knitting away while the heads tumbled down in front of her, Warren will sew up balls to keep occupied during matches.

The Kerry Packer revolution in the late seventies was approaching when Warren got his Level 1 coaching certificate in Wagga. With little money in the kitty and a new wife to support, he couldn't splurge on a motel room when he drove to Sydney to do his Level 2, so for a couple of days he slept in his little car in the grounds of Sydney University, where the course was held. Warren would wake up, gulp down some water from a bubbler and head off to the lectures. He did his Level 3 at the Village Green, home ground of the University of NSW club, at which he was appointed coach for the 2004/5 season. He flew to Sydney each Thursday morning for the game on Saturday and headed back to Wagga the next morning.

Warren has worked with elite players at the Adelaide Academy and with the Australian Under 17s and 19s, and as a batting and fielding coach with NSW Pura Cup players. At the other end of the scale, for thirty years he was NSW Cricket's Development Officer in the Riverina, travelling up to 60,000 kilometres a year to oddly named places such as Tooleybuc and Merriwagga, along roads with potholes that would swallow a Mini, past the corpses of kangaroos and across creeks on precarious single-lane bridges. Once Warren was disturbed by an overtaking emu pecking on the back window of his car as he drove along. Yet he would rather tootle through vast expanses of silent nothingness than tackle the Sydney traffic, which he hates. He works at places with no nets and no fence, just a wicket in the middle. If a ball is hit off the playing area, the fetcher has to keep an eye peeled for black snakes.

In his unending search to unearth another star cricketer, Warren went to a fitness camp at Borambola, some twenty-seven kilometres from Wagga, where a very polite youngster from Albury who, like Warren, had red hair and freckles, caught his eye. There was something about Dominic Thornely. He wasn't the most talented pupil that day, but he followed Warren around listening intently to every word. Warren recalls: 'Dominic was about thirteen and quite tall, and although most tall young blokes can be a bit clumsy, he was an athlete who probably could have played AFL.' Since that day Dominic has been a disciple of Warren's batting and fielding drills. In the 2004/5 season, he emphasised his talent by whipping up an unbeaten 261, with an Australian record eleven sixes, for NSW against Western Australia, figuring in a last-wicket stand of 219 with Stuart MacGill. At the end of the season Thornely was off to Pakistan with Australia A.

WARREN'S WAY

They still talk about the day Warren Smith was interviewed for a coaching job with Cricket NSW. Invited to sit at the head of the table in the board room, he looked at the suited, stern-faced selection committee. 'This looks like a meeting of the Mafia,' he chuckled. 'Where's the horse's head?' He got the job.

Warren suffered his first heart attack in 2001 while helping the lady next door move some wood on his return from a long bike ride. He felt dizzy, collapsed and was rushed to hospital. It flashed through his mind how his father had died. The last thing Warren heard was his wife Pam sobbing and her words, 'Please save him.' Thankfully, the doctors got Warren through, inserting two stents so there would be a full flow of blood through the valves of his heart. 'I had to make some changes,' Warren says. 'I really had to rest and not lift things but I can't sit back when I'm coaching. I have to be full on. I think you've got to be. My passion is that I love it and I love to see people do well.'

Three years later heart attack No 2 happened. He collapsed at the top of a hill after a coaching session with University of NSW at the Village Green at Kensington and lay in the gutter for twenty minutes. He recovered, but when he got back to Wagga he collapsed again. They put in new stents and soon he was off and running, often going to the hospital to counsel fellow Wagga residents about how to cope with life after having a heart attack.

Warren likes to coach in game situations and insists that his training sessions and pre-game warm-ups are short and sharp. Pity help the shirker who doesn't throw himself into the drills whole-heartedly. Warren has been known to call an abrupt halt when things get sloppy and send the players on their way with the help of a few choice expletives. At University of NSW practices, all players must wear the club's gold T-shirts and black shorts to give them the feeling and look of a well-organised outfit that means business. Warren is uncompromising on dress standards on and off the field. One day as we sat watching University of NSW batting in a club match, he exploded, 'Look at that. It's a disgrace.' The opposing wicketkeeper's shirt was hanging out. Among the other no-nos are thongs and particularly doting mums and dads who carry their son's bag into the ground or, worse still, take them a drink on the field.

In his first season in the job, which he was urged to take by Michael Slater and club icon Geoff Lawson, Warren lifted University of NSW from near the bottom of the table to win the Sydney one-day series. They lost the three-day final of the premiership by one wicket to Sydney University, whom they had beaten in the one-day final. This was an extraordinary

Clues from Australian player Lisa Sthalekar at a Warren Smith coaching camp

achievement, as Sydney University's ranks included Test pair Stuart MacGill and Greg Matthews and three NSW Pura Cup players.

As a reward, the University of NSW sent the team on a tour of India, and Warren, with five thousand Wazza balls in his luggage, quickly found that his fame had preceded him. With the cricket-crazy locals well aware that he was Michael Slater's coach, they fought among themselves to carry his bags. Perhaps it was the overwhelming heat or maybe rushing from one place to another, but midway through the trip Warren suffered a mild heart attack in Mumbai. Befitting the status of the man who coached Slater, he was rushed to the city's main hospital, given the same bed the Indian Prime Minister had occupied and attended by the PM's surgeon. 'I was petrified,' Smith recalls. 'I woke up the next day and had the feeling I was the only white bloke in a city of twenty million.' Then he looked out the window and saw hundreds of boys playing cricket in the park below and soon was critiquing their style.

After suffering a third heart attack, most people would become a veritable cardiac cripple, doing little more than potter about. Not Warren, who was soon back whizzing about the State on a schedule that would tire a man half his age. There were cricketers of all ages who needed help.

'Warren challenges players in a way that's exciting,' says Lisa Sthalekar, the Indian-born cricketer who's a fixture in the Australian women's team. 'He isn't in it for money or prestige, simply the genuine enjoyment of seeing each player succeed. We might be girls, but Warren doesn't hesitate to push us hard to become better players.'

Warren's virtues are the old-fashioned ones of honesty and hard work spiced with fun, and he may be seen to stand for the thousands of diggers who went in at Gallipoli or fought and swore in the trenches, and laughed at authority and stood by their mates to the end.

He adores his wife Pam, who has put up with it all for thirty-five years, his son Bradley, a radiographer who lives in England, his daughter Brylee and grand-daughters Isabella, Winter and Perri. The St George rugby league team and Geelong in the AFL, too. But perhaps Warren Smith is never happier than when working with youngsters in the hope of finding another Michael Slater.

Terry Smith

1

COACHING WAZZA STYLE

I've never worn the baggy green Australian cap — didn't come remotely close to it. But I did start Michael Slater on the way to winning one. I suppose I could have walked around in a T-shirt saying 'I Coached Michael Slater' and made a lot of money, but I'm not that sort of person. I just happened to be there at the right time. It was the same with my friend Johnny Lewis and his triple world boxing champion Jeff Fenech. One afternoon Jeff and a group of mates arrived at the Newtown Police Boys Club where Johnny was teaching. If he hadn't been there, Jeff probably would have walked out and their partnership would never have happened.

I don't think I'm a 'oncer' because I coach Dominic Thornely, another country boy who, barring injury, surely will play for Australia. There's so much talent out there in the bush in NSW, with Sir Donald Bradman, Bill O'Reilly, Stan McCabe, Alan Davidson, Doug Walters and Adam Gilchrist the cream of the crop.

Who, you might ask, is Warren Smith? I haven't played first class cricket, so what would I know? I don't claim to be the brightest spark around, because I left school at fourteen when my dad became very ill. Still, I'm a good listener and not much escapes me. I've picked the brains of some of the smartest men in cricket, soaking up every scrap of information like a sponge.

Without blowing up my own tyres, I think God has given me a gift of being able to communicate with people. I try to have fun with players and give them drills that are different to help them score more runs, take more wickets, hold more catches and save more runs in the field. I look outside the square but still stick rigidly to the basics. When you've been kicking around as long as I have, you know it's the only way, because a player who has mastered the fundamentals and knows why he does what he does will handle the pressure and make fewer mistakes. Apart from helping Slater and Thornely on their path to the top, I enjoy taking an average player and making him better. There are no secrets or short cuts. You must correct the fault after explaining to the player why it happens, rather than indulge in band-aid coaching which will not work long term. If you get the basics right, you're halfway there, providing you don't stifle a player's individuality and turn him into a robot.

YOU CAN'T KNOW IT ALL

I'm not one of those coaches who think they know everything about this wonderful game. I specialise in batting and fielding and leave the bowling to guys like Geoff Lawson. One of the problems when Australia lost the Ashes in 2005 was that the coach, John Buchanan, tried to do everything himself, and largely with his computer. But there are some things you can't fix with software, and he was reluctant to call in a specialist to stop the bowlers no-balling or get the batting back on track. It wasn't too hard to work out where the Australian batters were going wrong: their footwork was sloppy, their heads were outside the line of the ball, and at times their hands weren't in synch. If you haven't got nice hands, you'll never do any good.

Buchanan's critics claimed he didn't have the technical expertise to advise on the mechanics of batting and fast bowling, and were incensed by the way he allowed the fielding drills introduced by Bob Simpson to decline in quality and intensity. However, Ricky Ponting and Co bounced back the following summer, during which Buchanan brought in an American baseball coach to liven up the fielding and announced the appointment of Troy Cooley, the Australian who did an outstanding job coaching England's pace bowlers in the Ashes series, as coach of Australia's speed men.

Like John Buchanan, Cooley had a modest first-class career with Tasmania, but he provides further proof that great players do not necessarily make great coaches. Like myself, he likes to assimilate as much information as he can from the very best cricketers.

Buchanan's enthusiasm for the writings of Sun Tzu, the ancient Chinese warrior and philosopher, has puzzled many of the players, but I'm the last person to be critical of a man who tries something different. I've heard he has encouraged players to test their self-assurance by delivering talks to the rest of the team on subjects ranging from wrestler Hulk Hogan and the Bee Gees to the history of Ansett Airlines.

Of course there is a place for laptop coaching. You'd be a fool not to use computers, because they can help you score runs or take wickets by pinpointing weaknesses. Still, I like to be face to face with a pupil. Man to man or man to woman. It should be the simplest of games — you play with a ball and either bowl it, bat against it or try to catch or field it — but there's much more to it than that.

Computers played a crucial part in England regaining the Ashes in 2005. Every player in their squad had a laptop and at the end of each day of a match, a specialist analyst prepared an information package tailored to each player's needs, pinpointing problem areas and pertinent incidents of the day's play. England opener Marcus Trescothick, for example, is said to have checked on his laptop after each innings to discover whether he had overcome his previous reluctance to move his feet. In scoring well during the series, he was much lighter with his footwork. Just as importantly, computers gave them information about the opposing players. For instance, England had a clear and simple plan to curb Australia's danger man Adam Gilchrist: cut out his boundaries with sweepers on the rope while disrupting his favourite shots backward of point by attacking him from round the wicket to deny him room. Nullifying Gilchrist was the most important aspect of their Ashes victory, because he was the person who could have taken the game away from them.

And how do the English go about curbing a genius like Sachin Tendulkar? Like all batsman, the Indian hero is vulnerable early when he is still getting his eye in. During the initial attack, the English plan is for the bowler to aim to keep the ball just outside the off stump, forcing Tendulkar to prod at deliveries with the chance of providing a slip catch. However, it's suicidal to bowl anything on his legs. If this fails and

Tendulkar does get going, the strategy changes to containing his strokeplay. The best way to do this is to set a defensive ring of fielders with the aim of reducing the number of boundaries he can hit, and hope he plays a false shot.

I can see the time when, like tennis players and golfers, the top Australian cricketers will have a full-time private batting coach who comes under the umbrella of the No 1 coach. A fast bowling coach is a must, too. Our pace men bowled so many no-balls on the last Ashes tour because they were off balance, and a guy like Dennis Lillee or Geoff Lawson would have fixed that in no time. From Tiger Woods and Roger Federer down, every elite achiever in international sport knows that he or she needs the help of a personal coach to maintain their edge. Woods also performs with the assistance of a caddie who knows his game and has an eye for detail, so his advice can be invaluable.

THE BUSINESS OF COACHING

Coaching is all about *why*. Why players are making mistakes and why certain adjustments must be made to make them more capable players. Bob Simpson, a hugely successful Australian coach, points to an old Chinese proverb that if you give a man a fish it will feed him for a day, but teach him to fish and you feed him for life. Cricket coaching is a bit like that.

I believe in short, sharp training sessions that have enough innovative drills to make it fun and interesting. If it's noisy and bubbly, the players are enjoying it. When Dominic Thornely invited me to Waitara Oval for a session with the local kids, I got some of them to throw balls down from the big trees beside the grandstand. Some of the balls hit seats and the fence and the boys were diving about catching them coming from all angles. I did that because cricket is a game of angles.

When I'm doing batting drills, there are only two things I really worry about — ball and feet. The ball comes and your feet go. That's all there is — ball, feet. Then I work my way through the rest of it. Get a tape of my schoolboy hero Neil Harvey in action and you'll see twinkling footwork that would delight the cricketing gods.

Just because I've got red hair and freckles, people might think I'm a cranky old so-and-so. I admit I can be the maddest bloke out there — until we get down to business. The guys know that when it's on, it's on. For instance, it's got to be quality, not quantity when it comes to throwdowns. I would rather throw twenty good balls at you than ninety-three rubbish balls. That way you get something out of it.

I try to have a crate filled with a hundred balls at every training session. It's like a golfer who hits a steady stream of practice balls to perfect his shots. A batsman has to have hundreds and hundreds of balls bowled or thrown at him and a bowler has to bowl hundreds of balls to get his stamina up. However, laps of the oval are out.

PLAYING THE MIND GAME

Cricket is a mind game, a bit like chess. You try to find out how smart the other person is. Early on in a game I like my fielders to have a throw back to the keeper. Even if the batsman is in his crease, throw it back. It helps build the pressure. Ricky Ponting complained about England doing this in the 2005 Ashes series, but Australia had been doing it for years. What about the time Ponting himself threw one back and hit a bloke?

Everyone's nervous out there on the cricket field. When the bowler runs in, he's nervous and the man at the batting end, he's nervous too. You've got to be prepared to stand up and be the one who breaks the shackles. Cricket is character-building because it's the greatest cut-throat game of them all. You can be down a goal in soccer, a try in rugby, a set in tennis and still have a chance of winning, but in cricket, once you're out, you're out. You've got to be philosophical, too. Everybody drops a catch at some stage because we're all human and it's going to happen. There's nothing better than getting back to the shed after winning, but you can't win all the time and a loss can be character building. Don't forget that Sir Donald Bradman, the greatest player who ever lived, got out for a duck in his final Test innings.

I want the older blokes who have been through the mill to chat with the younger players and pass on tips while sitting in the dressing room. I also encourage the young guys to learn about the culture of the game. We all know about Bradman, but what about Jack Hobbs and an old English bloke with a beard named Dr WG Grace? Dr Grace is said to have played by his own set of rules. One year he called to a young batsman to toss him the ball back, then appealed for handling the ball and got him out!

One day a few years ago I went to a NSW team training session when David Sincock was manager of the Blues. When I told one of players that David had been a mesmerising spin bowler for Australia, he replied, 'Gee, I didn't know he played cricket.' It's interesting how much a coach can learn about the character of his players just from chatting with them in the dressing room on a rainy day.

COACHING THE GIRLS

Women cricketers mightn't have the strength and power of the men, and even though the ball they use is a smaller one, they're playing the same wonderful game. They need the same skills, so I coach them in exactly the same way as I would their male counterparts, though with fewer expletives perhaps.

Kids will be kids and girls can be a bit giggly when they're starting off, but if you're pretty firm and say we'll do this and do that, after a while they get the message. It's part of the deal. You don't back off and they appreciate that because they want to do well.

We do the same drills, with special emphasis on learning to work the ball, and when girls get to the stage where they can play a bit, they can be better listeners than some of the blokes. Many of them have been good hockey players, which helps sharpen their hand–eye coordination.

Our top women cricketers work as hard on their skills as the men and are getting better and better. The TV coverage of the Australian women winning the World Cup in South Africa was vibrant proof of this. A few of them could possibly play second grade against the men at some clubs, and I think Belinda Clark, the former Australian captain, might have gone close to playing first grade.

When they get to the top level of the game, the women want to be trained hard, and since the girls became integrated with Cricket Australia they have been able to tap into the best coaches and facilities like the Centre of Excellence in Brisbane. They go to the gym, run, swim and even do yoga. Lisa Keightley, who once hit a Test century at Lord's, is now coaching the NSW Breakers in a full-time role, a huge breakthrough for women coaches.

It's the same in women's hockey and basketball. The Hockeyroos have won Olympic gold and the basketballers made an Olympic final since the Australian Institute of Sport got behind them. Lauren

Jackson has become a superstar in American women's basketball.

When coaching the cricketing girls, don't go soft on them. They want to be pushed because they know it will help them be competitive. Anyone who tries to compare Karen Rolton with Ricky Ponting, Cathryn Fitzpatrick with Brett Lee and Lisa Sthalekar with Shane Warne would be overdosing on magic mushrooms, but there is still an important place for women in the game of cricket. I love helping them. They've come a long way since Sir Leonard Hutton said women's cricket was a bit like watching a man knit.

Even though Zoe Goss once dismissed the great Brian Lara at the SCG in a charity game in 1995, I am totally opposed to women playing against men. We had a girl in Wagga called Julie Stockton, who represented Australia and used to play first grade against the men. One day she opened the batting against a side I was captaining, and I said to the bloke with the new ball, 'If she hits you for four, I want you to go after her.' When he said he didn't want to hit her, I told him, 'If she wants to come out here, she plays like anybody else. Just remember, if she belts us around for fifty, we've got to chase those runs.'

MANAGING PEOPLE

My pet hate when I'm coaching kids is the father who tells me his son is going to be another M.J. Slater. The boy gets embarrassed. If the parent wants to stand at the end of the net, I ask him to leave so I've got full control of his son. I can't stand to see a parent carrying a boy's bag into the ground or a kid jumping the fence and coming in to bat from where he was sitting with his mum and dad.

With kids, you can expect the unexpected. For example, Mike Hussey, who jumped into the spotlight with such devastating effect in the summer of 2005/06, was a right-handed bat until he watched Allan Border batting on TV. He liked what he saw and from that day the Western Australian faced up to the bowler in a left-handed stance.

There's so much cricket today at the top level, with players switching from one-day to four- and five-day games and wanting to hang around for a lot longer because of the dollars involved. So the coach must be a people manager as much as anything, particularly to deal with the burnout factor.

My favourite saying to Michael Slater before he batted in a second innings after failing in the first, or when he came off after surviving a dropped catch was, 'Make the buggers pay.' It can be a pretty nasty world out there, and people are going to try to cut you into little pieces. You've got to back yourself, because if you don't, who else is going to?

I try to teach all my pupils from Slater and Thornely down that people skills are just as important as cricketing skills and self-belief. Don't

SHOULD A COACH BE A SELECTOR?

Absolutely not. The coach certainly should make recommendations to the selectors, but a player might have reservations about confiding in his coach about a problem if the coach sits on the selection panel. Bobby Simpson struck problems with this during his highly successful stint as Australian coach.

ever forget your roots, I tell the boys. Remember the little old lady who gave you a drink of water or the gentleman who drove you to a cricket match.

Players respond differently to being coached. Some accept advice and criticism better than others. Some resent it, others lap it up, but there's a danger that they are so desperate to learn that they grab every bit of advice that's going. Early in his career, Justin Langer listened to so many people that he became confused, but he learned to become selective about what to adopt.

It was the same thing with Michael Slater in one-day cricket. We often spoke about why he wasn't any good at it, and I think it was because he got confused by too many people in his ear telling him what to do. After all, he played Test cricket like a one-day player. How many times did Slater destroy a Test attack in the first session of play? The stats show that practically every time he scored a century it set up an Australian victory. I can recall him hitting the South African quick Alan Donald over cover for six at the Melbourne Cricket Ground, which is no mean feat.

Enthusiasm is undoubtedly one of the main assets of a good coach, and I get an enormous kick out of being involved and contributing to the game with my hands-on style, which tries to get away from mechanical, boring drills. I love to see players I'm coaching have a smile on their face. If Michael Slater was smiling I knew he was going to do well, but once he got that grumpy old man look, he was going to play like one.

2

BATTING BASICS

'Batting is a major trial before an eleven-man jury.'

Richie Benaud

In batting, the worst thing you can do is over-coach and turn a player into a robot. There is no point in overloading the brain. He's only got one ball coming at him, so it's fatal if he's thinking of half a dozen things. When a bloke nicks a ball, I hate to see him walk away to square leg muttering to himself. He's angry and you can almost see him going through the checklist. I'd rather see him take a few deep breaths and face up to the bowler with a smile on his face. That way he's more relaxed.

If a player has natural ability, don't try to change it. Develop and strengthen the talents he or she already possess. While still insisting on sound technique, allow their individuality to come out rather than making them a slave to the orthodox method.

Champion batsmen come in all shapes and sizes, although there aren't too many tall players among them. Sir Donald Bradman, Allan Border, Sachin Tendulkar, Sunil Gavaskar and Brian Lara are comparative tiny tots who have dominated the world's finest bowlers. It is no coincidence that each of them are or were nimble on their feet, enabling them to get quickly into position or duck underneath a delivery that would trouble a taller man. Having said that, the taller batters have the compensation of a big reach, which gets them further forward to spin.

Technically, Bradman, Border and Sir Garfield Sobers were hardly models for a coaching manual because so many of their methods were unorthodox. But no matter. Bradman produced shots that were beyond the reach of any player who ever picked up a cricket bat, while Border's concentration and wonderful eye paved the way for 11,174 Test runs and a further 6524 in one-dayers, many of them against the fireballs of the West Indies. I'm told that, as a coach, Sobers tried to get players to bat like him, which was an impossibility.

TIP

'What distinguishes a good player from an average batsman is that the good player watches the ball all the way down the pitch. The average player watches it four-fifths of the way. Even if your technique is poor, if you keep watching the ball in that last little half yard, you can still get out of trouble.'

Murray Creed, former South African provincial player now in the NSW squad.

FIRST THINGS FIRST

I don't care what anyone says, the first thing a batsman must have is defence, because without it he's not going to be in long enough to do any good. Once a player has got his defence right, I develop the rest of his game, working through the off-side and on-side strokes and then the horizontal shots.

Players must aim to be equally proficient going forward on the front foot and back on the back foot, but must never go backward or forward before the ball leaves the bowler's hand. You've got no hope if you play this dangerous guessing game. And don't simply bat from the crease. 'Go right back or right forward,' Sir Vivian Richards, the champion West Indian, used to say. 'Use as much of the crease area as possible.' But this cannot be done without the correct footwork. If you straddle the crease, it's almost impossible to play the ball with the full face of the bat. Like when hitting a golf shot, you've got to keep your head still to ensure you're balanced when you strike the ball. If you're off balance, things go everywhere.

Another crucial thing is that the batsman must respect the bowler. You'll see guys who go after the bowlers helter skelter and try to belt them, but unless you're a freak like Adam Gilchrist this is fraught with danger. Look at what happened to Matthew Hayden. He was hitting little blokes who couldn't get the ball much higher than a bail all over the place, but when he tried to do that against England in 2005 he ended up fighting for his place in the side. Hayden changed his tempo, put more emphasis on defence, and the result was back-to-back hundreds against the Poms and the World XI.

GRIP

The grip on the bat is a prime consideration because the hands have to work together. It must allow you to be flexible, mixing powerful drives with strokes requiring soft hands. The hands are kept close together towards the top of the handle, with the V between the thumb and forefinger of the top hand directly above the corresponding V of the bottom hand.

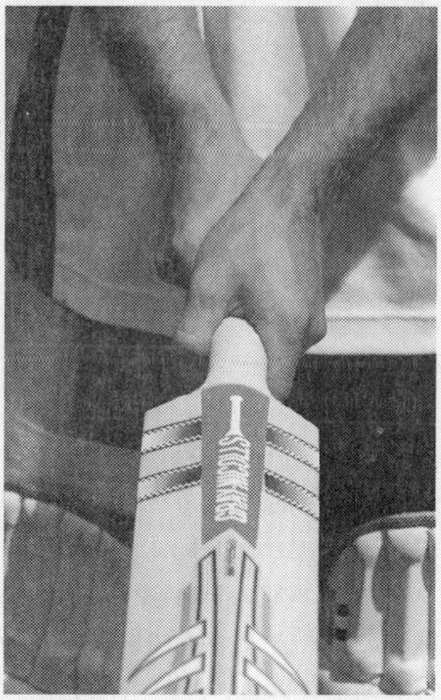

The classic left-hand grip

Of course, not all grips are the same. Adam Gilchrist grips the bat higher up the handle than any of the other top players in the world. This has the effect of increasing his power because it expands the arc in which he swings, but is not why he first tried such a grip when advised to by a coach at the Australian Academy in Adelaide as a teenager. It simply felt so comfortable that he stuck with it.

When Sir Donald Bradman came down from the bush in the twenties, he was told by one of the

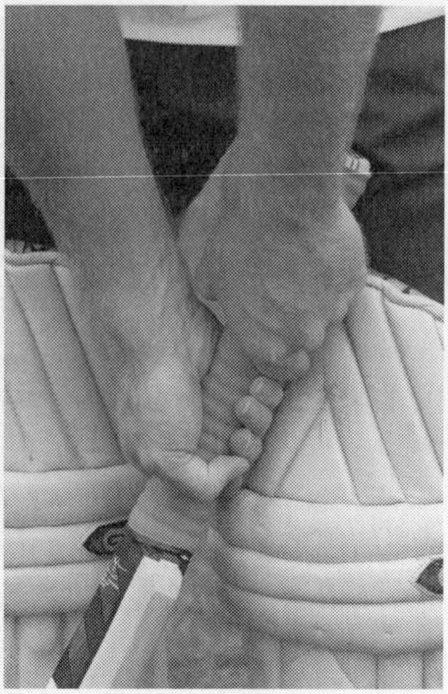
Right-hand grip

NSW State coaches that he must change his grip. Most country boys would have accepted such advice but Bradman said no. Like Frank Sinatra, he did it his way. When Greg Chappell was young, he was taught to hold the top hand more to the front of the bat, and while this was fine for leg-side shots it restricted his strokes on the off side. When Bradman advised the teenaged Chappell to change his grip so that the top hand was more towards the back of the blade, the suggestion was happily accepted. After much work, the change resulted in a fuller swing-through of the blade for his off-side strokes.

If the bat is gripped low, it brings too much bottom hand into play, which can cause a batsman to play a lot of balls in the air. The top hand is usually the weakest hand, so I have a drill where the player, wearing pads and gloves, runs the length of a pitch with the top hand holding the bat out in front. The upshot is that as your innings progresses past fifty, the arm doesn't start to get tired.

One more thing: if your hands are not relaxed, you'll probably bring too much bottom hand into the shot. Don't strangle the handle of the bat.

STANCE

When you sit in a car, you must be comfortable if you're going to drive it properly. So, when batting, adopt a comfortable, relaxed stance that allows you to go forward or back, or get your hips going in the rotation needed for other shots.

The feet are parallel to the crease to enable you to stay sideways to the bowler, with the weight equally distributed between the feet, and the feet no further apart than the width of your shoulders. The toe of the bat rests behind the back foot and the left shoulder points down the pitch.

Of course, not every great player follows each of these guidelines. Garry Sobers batted with his feet close together, Don Bradman and Keith

Miller faced up to the bowler with the bat between their feet, and Andrew Flintoff stands with his feet wide apart and the bat resting between them. How does the Englishman get away with such unorthodoxy? Simple. Flintoff combines a wonderful eye with brute strength and looks to have a big, wide bat when he plays forward. If his feet were closer together, he wouldn't be as effective. Flintoff is not nimble enough to use his feet like a smaller man, so he could get a bit off balance. However, while Flintoff's method works for him, it's completely contradictory to my philosophy of 'ball feet', which is all I've ever worked on. You either go forward or go back to the ball, and if your feet don't move, nothing does.

As the batsman faces up at the crease, his weight should be on the balls of his feet like a dancer, ready to transfer his weight from one foot to the other depending upon the length of the ball. According to Shane Warne, no-one judges length better than Sachin Tendulkar. Once the decision is made, he rolls onto the front or back foot with what he calls his 'floating' technique. Some players take a stance with the bat held a long way off the ground, notably Mike Brearley, Graham Gooch and Tony Greig. I've never liked this method because your hands can start moving everywhere. After all, we're playing cricket, not baseball.

Phil Jaques

Dominic Thornely

THE TONY GREIG/MIKE BREARLEY STANCE

The stance of holding the bat at knee height well before the ball is bowled was made famous by English captains Tony Greig and Mike Brearley. Greig, an exceptionally tall man, devised it as a method to combat the express yorkers of Jeff Thomson. Graham Gooch, the England opener, was another who adopted this ploy in mid-career.

Greig, at 6 ft 7 in the tallest cricketer to captain England, was a very good player of spin but had trouble coping with Thomson's yorkers, so he changed his method and waited for the ball with the bat raised off the ground, ready to bring it down as necessary.

I'm happy to say that Sir Donald Bradman shares my distaste for this method. He told me: 'I would never have a bar of the Greig/Brearley stance, à la Statue of Liberty. In my book, a recipe for disaster because it ruins balance and rhythm. No wonder Brearley never made a Test hundred in the whole of his career.'

Brearley once claimed that he hummed a few bars of Beethoven as Dennis Lillee swept up to the bowling crease. He would wait with bat raised during Thommo's run-up and then lift it still further before the ball was released. His head simply had to move, and it's a cardinal rule of batting that your head has to be still.

Norm O'Neill had a great stance and Bobby Simpson was very relaxed at the crease. Michael Clarke's stance reminds me of Mark Waugh, who was very elegant as he faced up to the bowler. The kids today should watch Tendulkar and Brian Lara if they want a model to copy. Certainly not Marcus Trescothick, the Englishman. I know he's a Test player but his feet seem anchored to the ground.

As Don Bradman used to say, the stiller you can keep yourself at the crease before the ball is bowled the better. Simon Katich shuffles about a lot and it seems to work for him, but if you fire a rifle and your head is moving, where's the bullet going to go? It's common sense.

TAKING GUARD

Should you take guard on middle stump, middle and leg, or leg stump? Remember that it's crucial to know where your stumps are, particularly the off stump. I always reckon a young player should take centre because he or she will have good eyes. Of course, it's the oldest trick in the book to ask for leg stump and bat on middle, but umpires aren't silly — they know you're only trying to escape being given out leg before.

If you bat a bit chest-on and the eyes aren't as sharp as they once were, it might be an idea to try batting leg stump. There's a blind spot down the leg side, but if the ball is outside your legs and you're batting leg stump, you know you can work it away without any danger. However, when you bat leg stump, you must get your foot right across to the off or there could be a gap for the ball to go through.

When you're batting, you own the crease and must try to use every bit of it. Steve Waugh was the best I've seen at getting right back to play a short ball, and his secret was that he knew exactly where his off stump was.

BATTING OUT OF YOUR CREASE

Playing against bowlers who were struggling to get a ball over bail height, Matthew Hayden got away with batting out of his crease for a long time, until England sorted him out in 2005. Imagine trying that against the quicks in the great West Indies sides led by Clive Lloyd and Sir Vivian Richards. If they didn't kill him, they'd have pinned him to the sightboard like a butterfly. If one of their first three fast bowlers didn't get him, the fourth one would.

I don't like to see players batting out of their crease. However, I know if you're getting tied down by a medium-fast bowler it can help break his grip by moving a couple of feet outside the crease to turn length balls into half volleys or full tosses. However, don't go forward too much or you'll find yourself caught in no man's land.

BACKLIFT

Some coaches suggest the batsman should take the bat back directly over middle stump, but the best players have never done that. It's more natural to pick up the bat towards first or even second slip, as great batsmen from Bradman down have done.

Backlift

Most openers use a shorter backlift early in their innings to avoid being beaten by sheer pace. Greg Chappell did the same when he got to the crease. I can't see the point in having a high backlift against the quicks. About half a backlift, I'd say. Phil Jaques, the opener who won his first Test cap against South Africa on Boxing Day 2005 as a reward for scoring buckets of runs for NSW in the Pura and ING Cups and in the English county championship, is among the players who await all bowlers with his bat raised above the ground.

FORWARD DEFENCE

The forward defensive stroke is played to a straight, good-length ball which is too short to drive but too far up to allow a back-foot shot. The main thing is for the eyes to be over the top of the ball. Lead with the head and front shoulder and, with the knee *bent*, place your front foot as close as possible to the pitch of the ball. The top hand is in control, with the bottom hand holding the bat softly. Play the ball with an angled bat as close as possible to the front pad so the ball cannot slip through. As with everything in batting, balance is the key. The front knee must be bent, because if you stand stiff-legged your head can't get over the ball. Sachin Tendulkar provides a perfect model for this shot, as he gets right over the top of the ball in the manner of Bradman. Brian

The top hand controls the forward defensive shot by Dominic Thornely and Phil Jaques

Back-foot defence

Lara is another with the perfect technique for the forward defensive stroke.

BACK-FOOT DEFENCE

To counter a short-pitched delivery in line with the stumps but not short enough for an attacking shot, step back and across with the back foot, your head in line with the ball. Standing at your full height, stay sideways by keeping the back foot parallel with the crease. The front leg naturally draws back to join the back leg. Stay side-on to present a narrow target. The head *must* be over the ball and the bottom hand soft and comfortable, with a raised front elbow keeping the bat straight and in control of things. Steve Waugh should be used as a model for back-foot defence.

THE COVER DRIVE, OFF-DRIVE AND STRAIGHT DRIVE

Dominic Thornely's lofted drive

These shots are played to an over-pitched ball or half volley, with the head and front shoulder leading the way and the front foot following. With a full swing of the bat, the foot, knee, elbow and shoulder point the same direction the ball is to go. The hitting zone is just in front of the front foot, with the bat making a complete follow-through in the direction you want the ball to go. The top hand remains in control and the head is kept still as contact is made with the full face of the bat. All good players excel with such a stroke because it's in their V.

For a cover drive, the left toe points towards cover, with the blade a fraction open at contact. This shot should be played to balls pitched well clear of the off stump. Among the modern-day Australian players, nobody hits a cover drive better than Mike Hussey, who strikes the ball with grace, power and balance.

The lofted drive is another potent attacking stroke. Using a full follow-through, you can play it from the crease or by advancing down the wicket with nifty footwork, with the ball struck earlier or a little further beyond the front foot. As with a golf shot, the head must stay down.

Michael Slater watches the ball like a hawk
Newspix/Phil Hillyard

THE ON-DRIVE

The on-drive is played to a ball over-pitched on leg stump. The secret is to place the front leg *outside* the line of the ball. Bend your knee to keep your weight forward and the ball on the ground. Too much bottom hand and you will play across the line. Greg Chappell was a master of this stroke. In a most elegant manner he got into position, stood up straight and played through the V with a full swing of the bat. Michael Slater was another to excel at the on-drive, almost running with the shot as he played it. When he hit one, it sounded like the crack of a rifle shot.

The on-drive

THE FORCING SHOT OFF THE BACK FOOT

This shot is played to a short-pitched ball. Stay sideways as the back foot is taken towards the stumps, with the bat controlled by the top hand and a high left elbow. The bottom hand adds power just as the ball is struck. Sunil Gavaskar, the Indian champion, loved this stroke.

The square cut

THE SQUARE CUT

Lots of runs come from this stroke, which is played to a short ball wide of the off stump. As you lift the bat, step back across the stumps with the weight on your back foot. With a turn of the front shoulder, throw the arms down and outwards from a high backlift to strike the ball at full arm's length. With head and eyes over the bat as it contacts the ball with a roll of the wrists, the body shifts to a bent back leg. Let the ball come to you rather than forcing the shot. The square cut was a signature stroke for Doug Walters, and Adam Gilchrist loves the shot.

THE LATE CUT

Played later in flight than the square cut and finer through the slips area, this shot isn't seen a lot today unless it's in the one-day arena. While the square cut calls for power, the late cut needs soft hands. As the ball is to be played behind you at the last moment almost in line with the stumps, watch it right onto the bat and make use of the speed of the ball. Sometimes it's whipped away almost from the gloves of the wicketkeeper. Sir Donald Bradman was a wizard at this shot, and Brian Booth another elegant exponent.

THE PULL SHOT

This horizontal, cross-bat stroke is used to pull a short-pitched ball to leg. Move the back foot back towards the stumps and allow the swing of the bat to open up the body so you end up chest-on to the bowler. The head must be kept still for as long as possible and the wrists rolled to keep the ball down. Try to strike it well in front of your body to avoid being cramped. With the weight finishing on the front leg, aim for square leg or mid-wicket. As his sharp eye picks up the ball so early, Ricky Ponting is the master of this stroke because he gets into position so quickly.

Ricky Ponting's pull shot

THE HOOK SHOT

Ideal for dispatching a high, bouncing ball from a fast bowler. Move back and across the crease inside the line, but beware if the pitch is supplying uneven bounce. This is another crossbat shot which calls for a high backlift and a full pivot to open up the body towards the bowler. Move inside the line of flight and aim to hit the ball down as square as possible on the leg side. West Indian cricketers are brought up to play the hook, with Viv Richards and Clive Lloyd notable exponents of the stroke. Many of the top 'hookers' are compact, powerful players with short backlifts.

THE LEG GLANCE

A delicate shot played to a delivery just outside the leg stump. The wrists are turned to use the pace of the ball to help it on its way. No power is needed, simply a sense of timing. Roll your wrists to the leg side and keep the ball down. Beware of glancing the ball too fine or playing the shot to a delivery too far away from the body, as the likely result will be a catch to the wicketkeeper.

THE SWEEP SHOT

The sweep is played to a slow delivery well pitched up outside or on the leg stump. The head leads the weight forward towards the line of the delivery. The front leg is bent, the head remains rock-steady and the ball is swept behind square leg by a horizontal bat. Unless the ball is wide, the front pad should be placed in line with the flight of the ball so the leg stump is not exposed. Matthew Hayden has scored heaps of runs with this shot.

The reverse sweep is high-risk rubbish. The great players shun it at all costs, particularly away from the one-day arena.

MOVING DOWN THE PITCH

Depending on the flight of the ball, leave your decision to move down the pitch to a slow bowler as late as possible so he cannot detect your intention. It's a risky business to decide to charge the bowler before he has bowled. Move the front foot forward and skip a step or two to the pitch of the ball, then play the same stroke you would employ from the crease.

WAZZA DRILLS — BATTING

All you need are stumps, bats, cricket or tennis balls, markers and batting tees. Pads are not required, but batters should always wear batting gloves so the hands become used to wearing them. Cricket or tennis balls may be used.

Using stationary batting tees, my drills are performed by players in front of their coach, who corrects errors in body movement. When a drill involves a moving ball, the coach may become the thrower or split the players into pairs. Either way, the role of the thrower is vital because a poor thrower will lead to a breakdown of drill quality. All throws should be underarm like a softball pitch, with the height and speed varied to simulate spin or pace bowling.

The batter must endeavour at all times to make contact with the ball on the half volley, hitting it along the ground to the defined marker or area. If performed well, the drills will improve a batter's speed and decision-making.

As drills are habit-forming, the coach should incorporate basic batting skill activities at each training session, particularly in the junior age groups. In all instances, players must strive to maintain a high quality in drill work as it is the cornerstone for what happens out in the middle.

PREPARATION

Right-hand batting stance

Left-hand batting stance

KEY LEARNING POINTS

- Eyes level
- Feet shoulder-width apart
- Side on — point shoulder to bowler
- Weight evenly distributed

PREPARATION (CONT'D)

KEY LEARNING POINTS

- Arms interlocked
- Rehearse front and back foot shots
- Weight transfer in 'rocking' direction

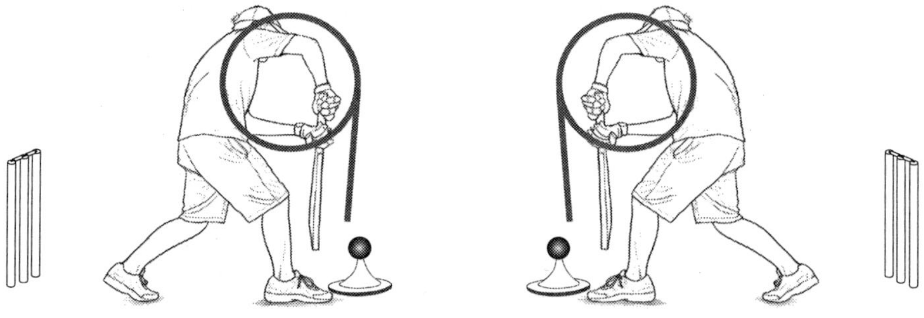

KEY LEARNING POINT

- Play shots using cricket bat and arms to form a '9'

FRONT FOOT DRILLS — STRAIGHT DRIVE

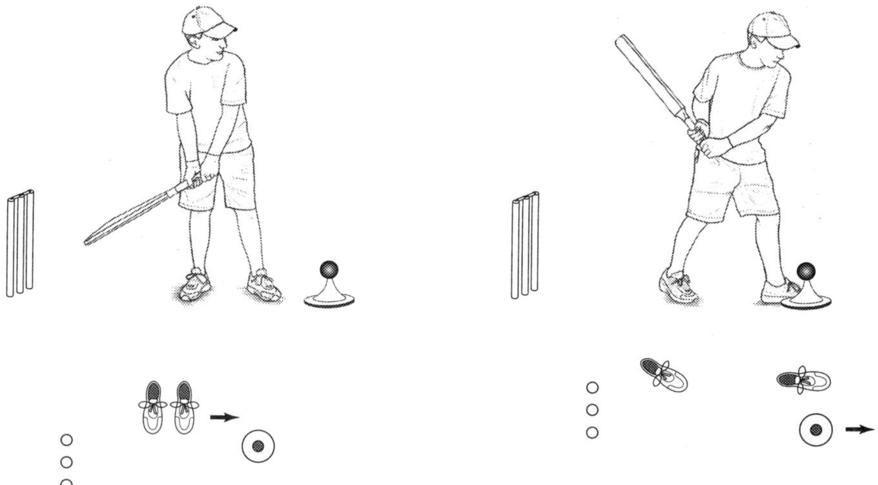

Right-hand batsman

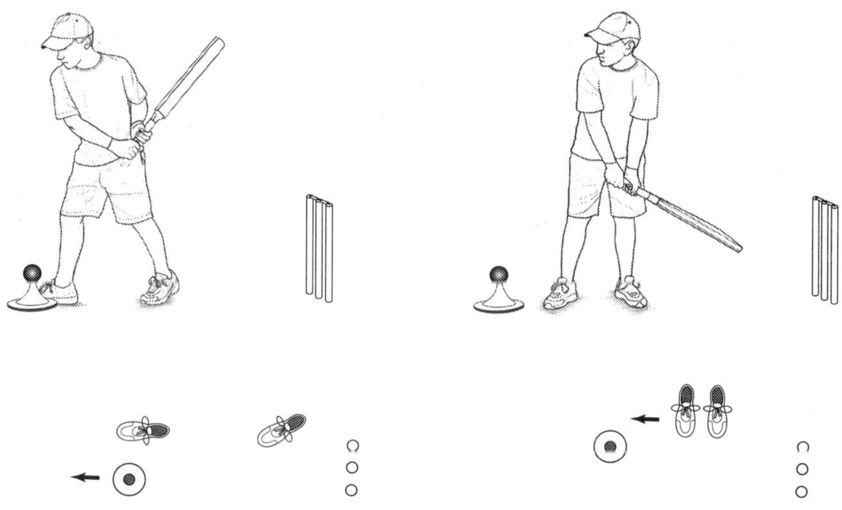

Left-hand batsman

KEY LEARNING POINTS

- Front foot to ball
- Back foot in walking position (raised)
- Head over ball
- Full face of bat at contact
- In batting, always remember: Ball — Feet.

FRONT FOOT DRILLS — COVER DRIVE

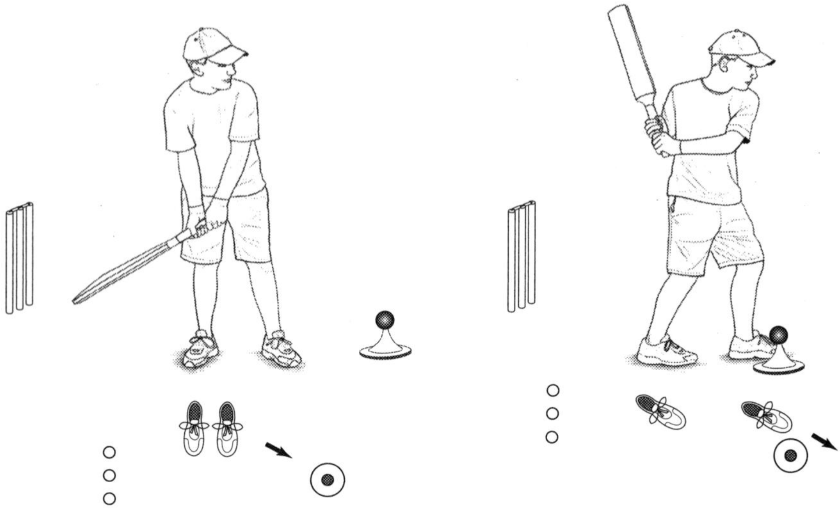

Right-hand batsman

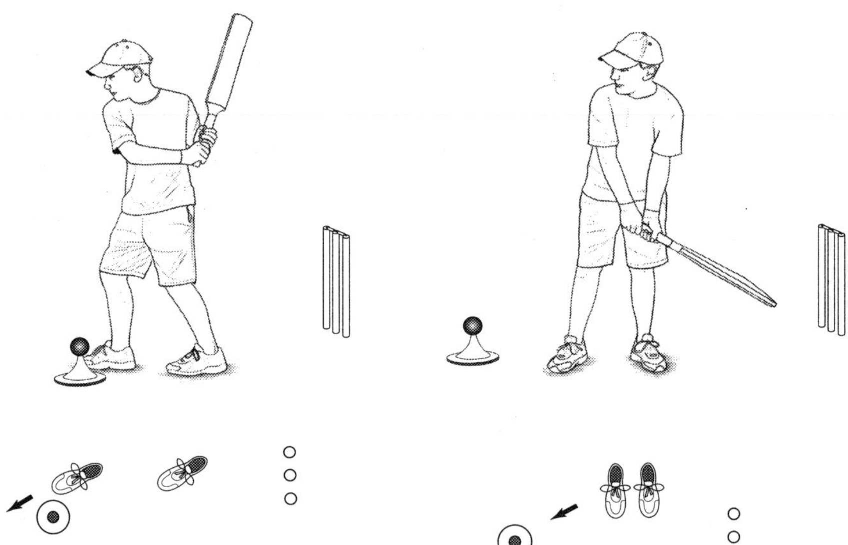

Left-hand batsman

KEY LEARNING POINTS

- Front foot points to intended direction of ball
- Balance at point of contact
- Head over ball

FRONT FOOT DRILLS — ON-DRIVE

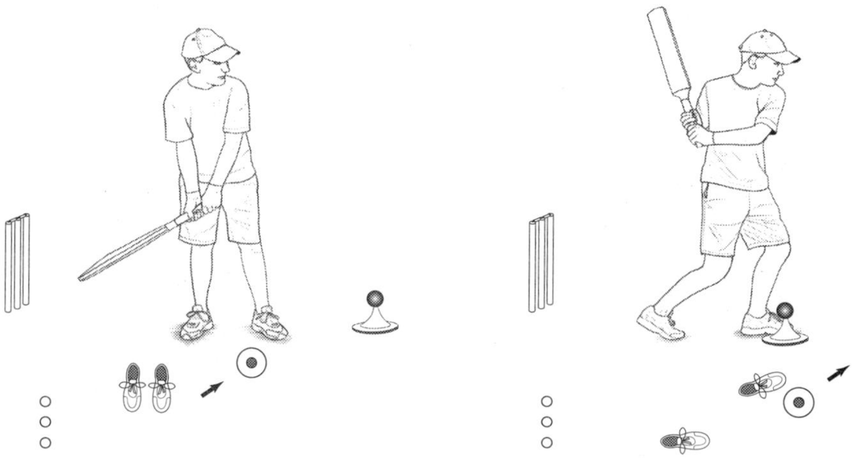

Right-hand batsman

Left-hand batsman

KEY LEARNING POINTS

- Move to the ball — do not 'open up'
- Front foot to leg side
- Maintain balance — do not fall away to off side

FOOTWORK

Positioned one stride down the pitch, I proceed to lob balls to the off side and on side. Footwork and balance are vital in these drills. Remember ball — feet as illustrated in the drop drills below.

Right-hand batsman

Left-hand batsman

KEY LEARNING POINTS

- Front foot close to pitch of ball
- Feet moving at different angles to ball
- Back foot position — 'walking'
- Turn a good ball into a bad ball through speedy footwork

FOOTWORK TO SPIN BOWLERS

Standing approximately two strides down the pitch from the batsman, the coach drops balls for the batsman to use speedy footwork to get to the pitch of the ball to play the on-drive, straight drive and off-drive, simulating the use of feet to spin bowling. Remember to make sure the front foot is always to the pitch of the ball.

Right-hand batsman

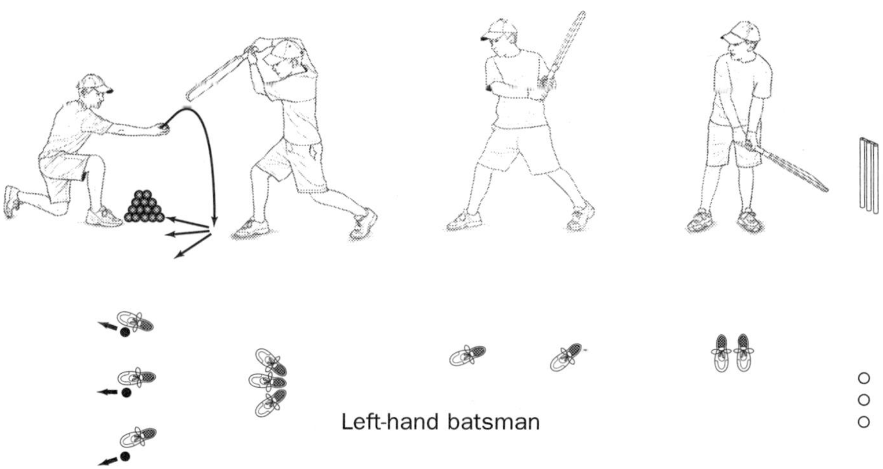

Left-hand batsman

- Vary the lob to increase footwork proficiency

FOOTWORK — HALF PITCH TO PACE BOWLING

Standing on an angle, the coach underarms the ball to the batsman from a distance of approximately 5 metres, making the batter take one, then two steps down the pitch to play off drives and on drives. If the batsman has difficulty getting to the lob, the coach can roll the ball. This will enable him to get his front foot to the pitch of the ball and hit through the line.

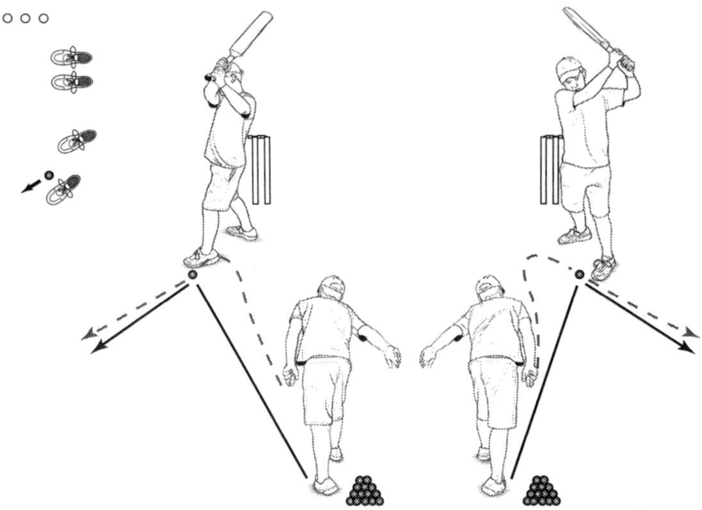

Right-hand batsman

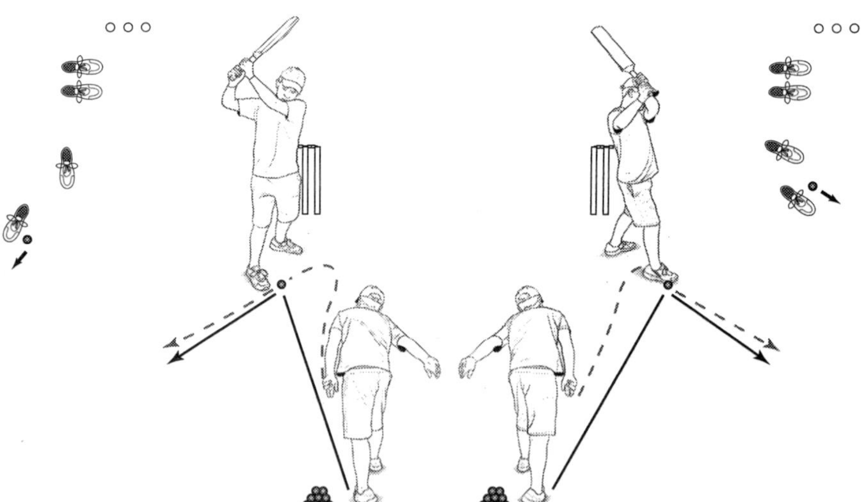

Left-hand batsman

Lob - - - - - - - - - Roll ————————

FOOTWORK — HALF PITCH TO SPINNERS

Coach bowls leg-spin from the middle of the pitch approximately 10 metres from the batsman. The batter is asked to play off-drives and on-drives with the emphasis on the batsman's foot being to the pitch of the ball. Markers can be used for reference points as illustrated below.

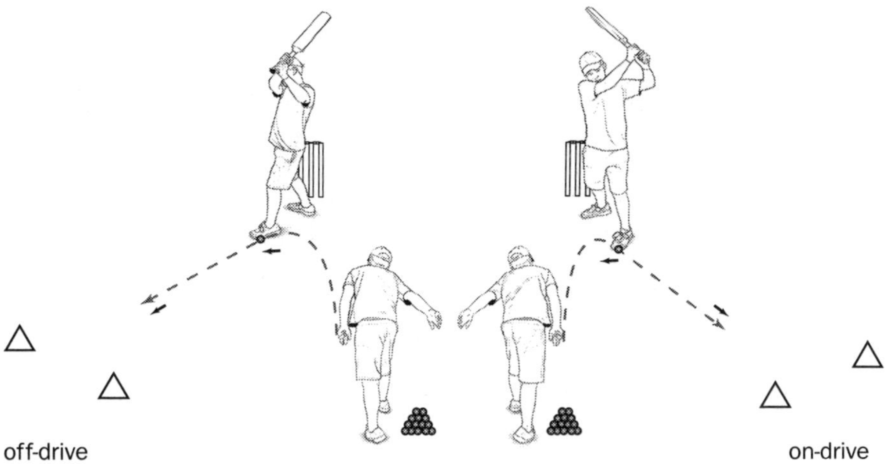

Right-hand batsman

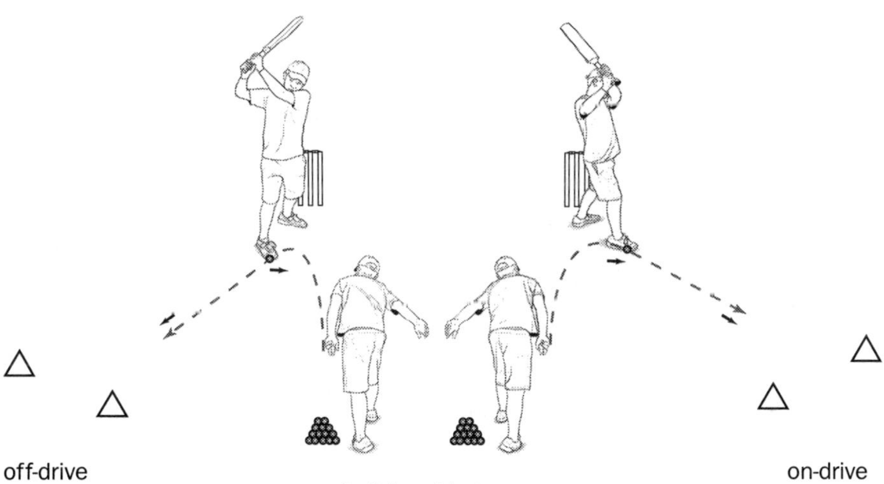

Left-hand batsman

THE SWEEP

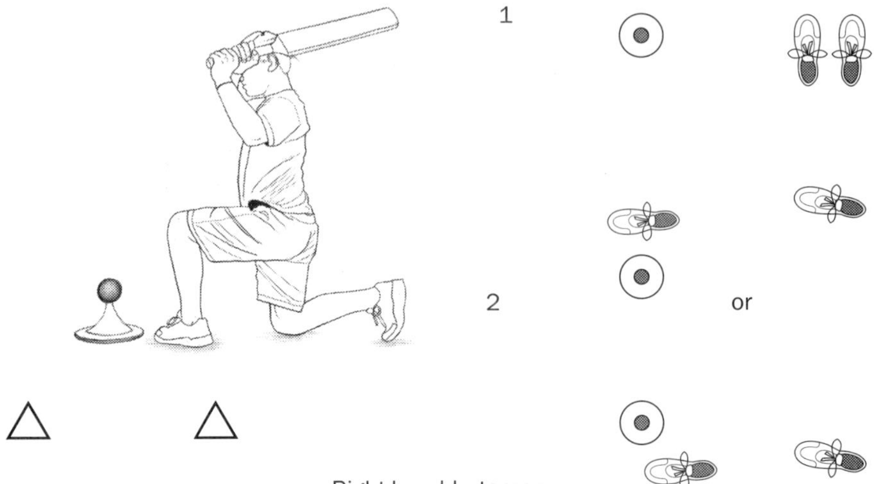

Right-hand batsman

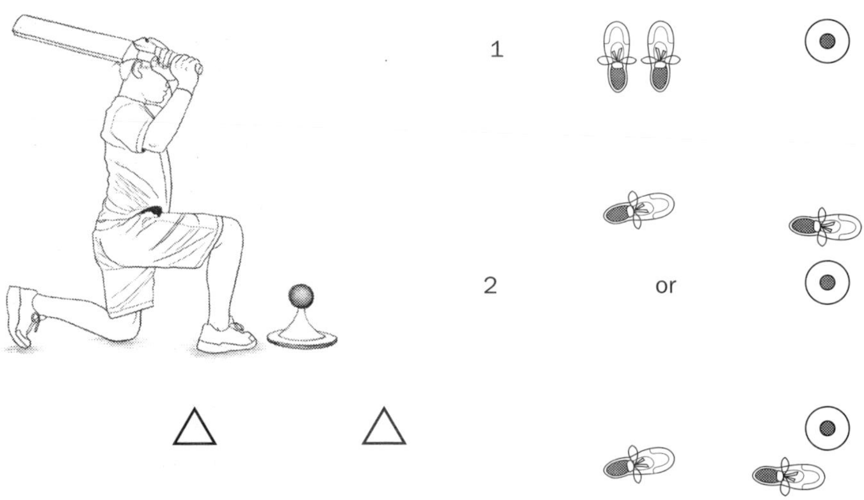

Left-hand batsman

KEY LEARNING POINTS

- Cover the line of the ball with pads
- Bat horizontal at point of contact
- Bring bat from high to low position
- Roll the wrists
- Weight should be forward
- Don't try to hit the ball too hard

THE BACK FOOT DRIVE

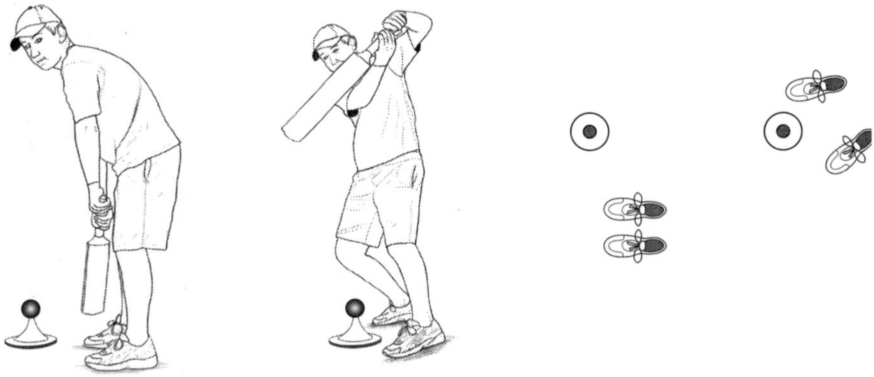

Right-hand batsman

Left-hand batsman

KEY LEARNING POINTS

- Stabilise back foot
- Head steady, eyes level
- Front elbow high at point of contact
- Full backswing

THE PULL/HOOK SHOT

Right-hand batsman

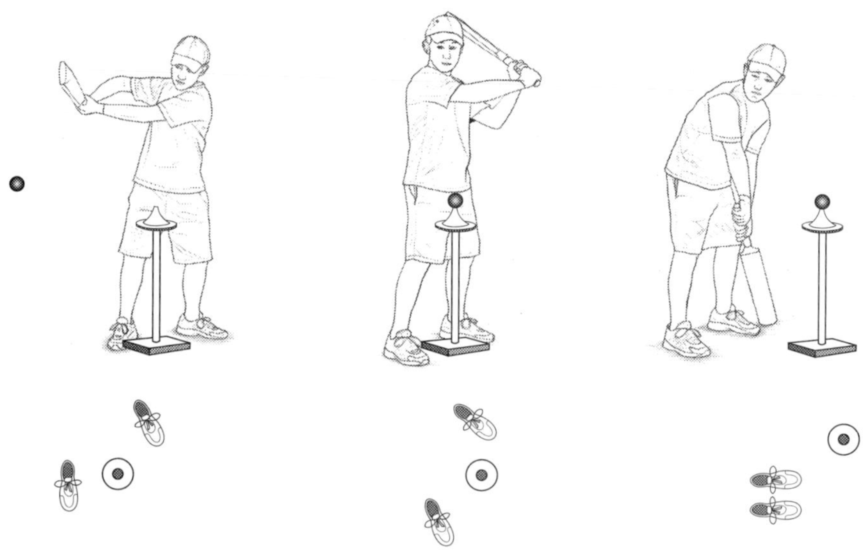

Left-hand batsman

KEY LEARNING POINTS

- Move back foot 'back and across' to off stump
- Body inside line of ball
- Hit down on ball — roll wrists

THE CUT SHOT

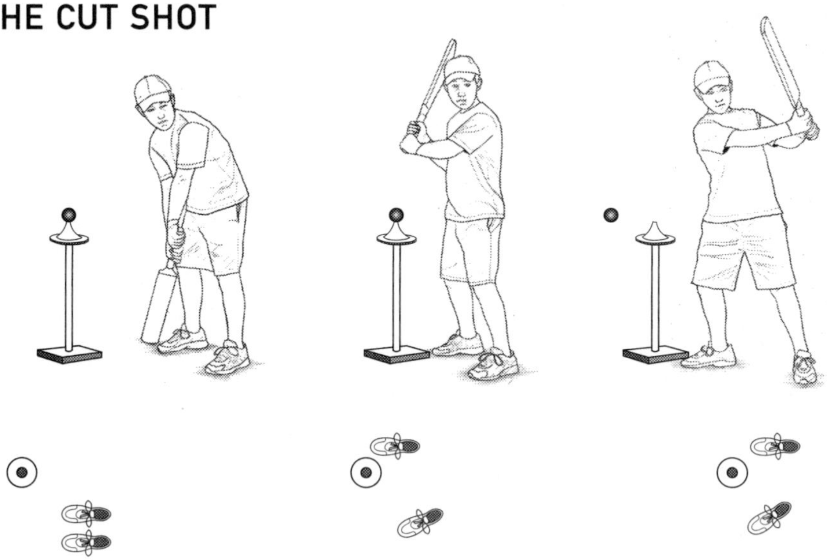

Right-hand batsman

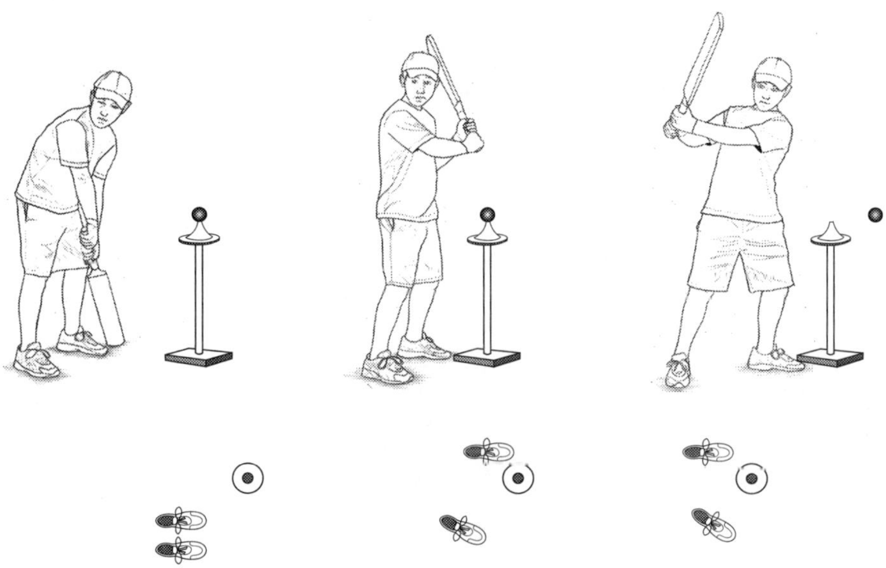

Left-hand batsman

KEY LEARNING POINTS

- Move back foot 'back and across' to off stump
- Head to line of ball
- Extend arms
- Hands high
- Lean towards the ball

BALL CONTROL

The ability to focus on the ball and control its speed and direction off the bat is an important skill for every batsman. In the following drills for a right-hander, it is important to ensure the bat remains horizontal and that participants are wearing batting gloves at all times.

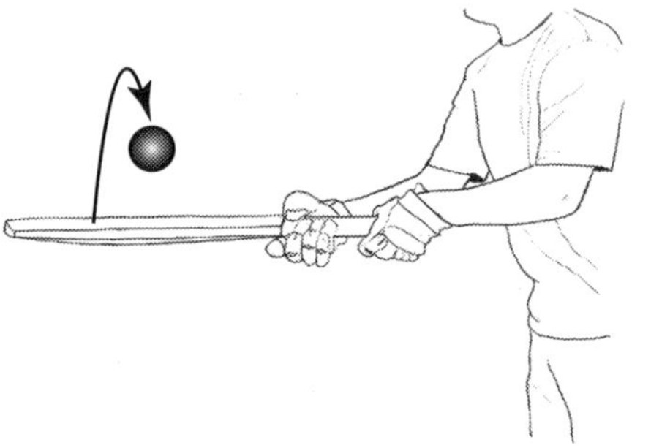

- Two-hand ball drill using bat face
- Batsman hits the ball with two hands positioned on the bat handle approximately 30 to 60 cm into the air off the bat

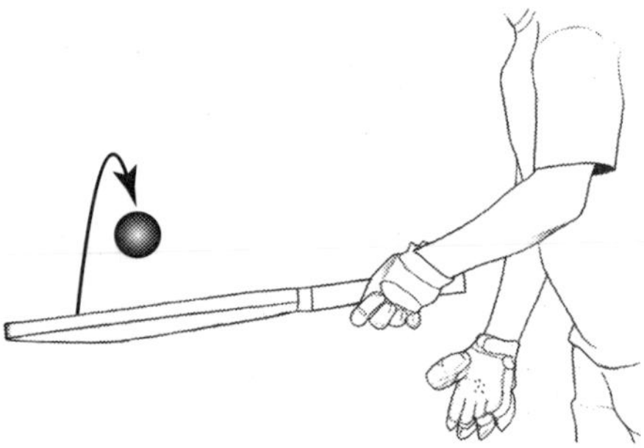

- One-hand ball drill using bat face
- Batsman hits ball with top hand positioned at the top of the bat handle approximately 30 to 60 cm into the air off the bat. Drill will improve control and develop wrist strength

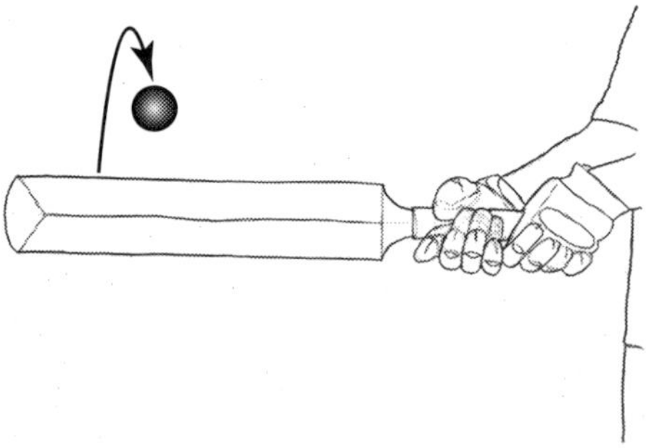

- Two-hand ball drill using bat edge
- Batsman hits the ball with two hands positioned on the bat handle approximately 30 to 60 cm into the air off the bat edge

KEY LEARNING POINTS

- Keep eyes on the ball
- Bat remains horizontal
- Maintain balance

BALL CONTROL RELAYS

Tap ball on bat face while walking then jogging between markers. Transfer ball to next player, keeping the ball off the ground. Hands to be in usual position on the grip, not on the bat face.

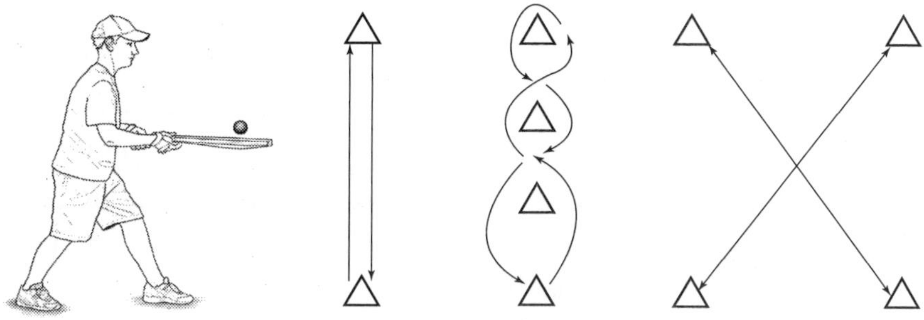

INCREASE DIFFICULTY BY:

- Placing markers at intervals in between to weave in and out
- Using one hand only
- Marker distance — Pitch length 20 metres

Players 'dribble' ball using a side skipping action (as if to come down the pitch to a spin bowler), maintaining control of the ball near their feet.

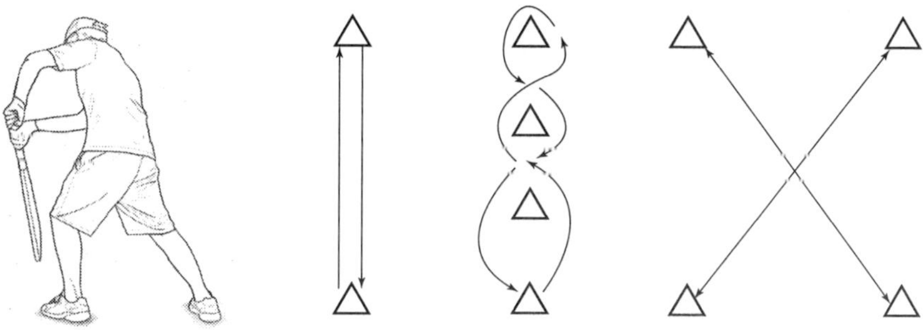

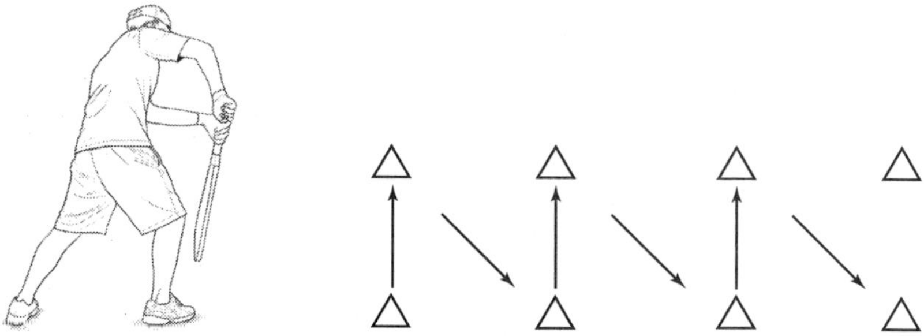

INCREASE DIFFICULTY BY:

- Introducing more balls
- Marker distance — Pitch length 20 metres

STRENGTHENING YOUR WEAK HAND

One of my favourite batting drills is for a player to strengthen his weak hand, the top hand on the bat, by running up and down a pitch length with the bat extended in front of him. As I like to simulate game situations, he must wear gloves and sometimes pads. Strengthening the weak hand gives a better balance, and players feel the difference when they get into the eighties or nineties. Lifting big weights is not the answer, because you use a bat weighing 2lb 8oz to 3lb in a game. You've got to build up to that.

3

BUILDING AN INNINGS

The secret of batting for a long time is to focus totally when it matters. It takes a particular mental attitude to play a long innings, calling for the batsman not to waste peak concentration. It takes time but you must learn to relax between deliveries.

Justin Langer's painstaking approach to preparing for an innings can begin well before the start of play. He will walk to the wicket and play a series of imaginary strokes from each end to the bowlers he's about to face, visualising what's going to happen later.

Few if any players are as meticulous as the Australian opener, but when you get to the ground be sure to take a look at the pitch. I've seen some people bounce a ball on it (if the curator's back is turned) to get a clue if it's bouncing high or low. I used to do it myself in the bush but now it's a no-no. However, a tap of the bat on the pitch can give a clue how it will play. For instance, if it's soft or damp, you know that most of your runs will come from the back foot with pulls and hooks. On the other hand it might be a fast, bouncy track. Spend time weighing up the options because if you're an opener the first few balls you face are crucial.

If you can't get to a net, have a team-mate do some throw-downs in the outfield so you can get your feet moving back and forward. In the dressing-room, you're best left alone before your innings. Time to have a think.

Unless you're an opener, watch the game as much as you can before going in to bat. Apart from checking out the bowlers and the pitch, look at the fielders. Which ones are slow and have a poor arm? They say Steve Waugh used to slip into tunnel vision mode to file all this data into the computer between his ears so that when he went in to bat, he was ready.

BE POSITIVE

When you walk out onto the ground, look up in the sky and have a little jog to get your legs going. Swing the bat and go from side to side. Get yourself ready to go, because you never know — the first ball could be a juicy full toss or a short ball to be hooked.

I want a batsman to have presence when he walks to the wicket. Who can forget the sight of Viv Richards strolling from the pavilion with an arrogant swagger, his maroon West Indies cap set at a jaunty angle? With a disdain for the world's swiftest bowlers, he refused to wear a helmet. It was his badge of pride. Clive Lloyd was another with genuine presence, while Steve Waugh's trademark was eagerness — he seemed to be almost halfway to the wicket as the umpire was replacing the bails. Watch Matthew Hayden when he gets to the crease. The Australian opener will squat on his haunches as he goes through his game plan one last time.

You'll be a bit nervous when you walk to the wicket, but too much of a negative attitude is fatal as it'll go through your batting and you'll get yourself out. You've got to have a bit of self-belief. When I was playing, I loved to feel the ball hit the middle of the bat straight away because if I was groping for it and my feet felt like elephant's legs, I was no good. However, once I got my feet going, I was all right. Footwork is so important, especially opening the batting.

Don't be scared by a name or a reputation. Of course, once a bowler has got a name as a bone-breaker or a big spinner, it can mess with your mind. There's an old saying that the batsman should play the ball, not the bowler. In other words, no matter who the bowler is, it's what the ball is doing by the time it reaches you that matters.

If you set out to play an innings in a defensive mode, you could miss out on some relatively easy runs, as by the time you realise the ball is there to be hit, the moment has gone. Worse still, trying to switch the game plan from defence to attack in mid-stroke is a sure-fire recipe for getting out.

SETTLE IN

Sir Donald Bradman always wanted to score a run off the first ball he faced because he liked to get straight into the game. But unless you're the Don, playing yourself in is vital. Get accustomed to the conditions of the wicket and the bowlers and let the runs flow naturally. There are very few players in the world who can take an attack apart from the first ball. Adam Gilchrist is the notable exception today, but Viv Richards was capable of doing it.

WAZZA TIP

SHOULD A BATSMAN WALK?

Adam Gilchrist walks and good luck to him, but I never did. It's a personal thing. Those who believe that a batsman should walk without waiting for the umpire to raise his finger say it's in the spirit of the game. I have no problem with the bloke who doesn't. Over a career you like to think that things balance out, with the times you get an edge and are given not out being evened up by the occasions you don't get a nick and look up and, to your horror, see the umpire raising the digit of doom. Brian Lara unfailingly accepts the word of an opponent that a catch has carried, whereas most players leave it to the umpire.

Don't get greedy. If there are overs in store, don't go out and blaze and blaze and blaze. I'm a great believer in a batsman milking the bowlers. Say you hit a four, then a two, a few dot balls and a single, you've got seven off the over, and if you're getting six or seven an over you're going to build your score. If you hit a couple of fours, drop back into the pace of the game for a few balls. There's not much point hitting three sizzling cover drives straight to a fieldsman and then playing a terrible shot and getting out. Why get out when there are forty, fifty or more overs to go?

SET MINI-GOALS

Setting mini-goals is a good thing, perhaps concentrating on getting to ten runs. Then another ten and another ten. Whatever suits you. History shows that you rarely find two batsmen in a partnership both scoring at a fast rate, so if one is going really well, the other feeds him the strike. If both players have the skill to play their role, the scoreboard ticks over.

Keep the ball on the ground until you get set and look for possible gaps in the field, working it into them. Singles can be run quickly, but above all, no flashy shots. It's frustrating for the bowler if every ball he bowls keeps hitting the middle of the bat, even if few runs are being scored.

RUNNING BETWEEN WICKETS

The humble single can be just as important as the majestically hit boundary because it rotates the strike and can force the bowler to change the line of his attack. If your partner is right-handed and you're left-handed, the captain needs to readjust the field, and as well as having to change his angle and bowl into a different channel, the bowler cannot get a full over to work on the batter's weaknesses.

Impudent quick singles annoy the opposition. Soften the hands and the ball will drop just in front of you. If your partner anticipates a single and is backing up at the non-striker's end, there's nothing the fieldsman can do to stop it. Be alert, though. Check where the fielders are standing, pick which hand they use to throw the ball, and look for the player with a weak arm.

Quick, clear calling is essential, with the striker calling for the run if the ball is in front of the wicket. It's the non-striker's call when the ball is behind the wicket. For a second run, the call is best left to the man who's running to the danger end. However, beware of turning blind.

Nobody likes fast bowling, and smart batsmen work the singles to rotate the strike to prevent the same player having to face six missiles in an over. This frustrates the speedballer, who is denied the chance to apply more pressure and force an error from the batter.

Back up from the bowler's end and, if there's a danger of being run out, slide the bat along the ground in front of you. Another aspect of the art of running is to conserve energy. In other words, it's ridiculous to run like Olympic sprinters for two when there's no chance of converting the shot into three. However, particularly in one-day cricket, run the first run quickly to put extra pressure on the fielder. He only has to fumble for a second and you've got him.

Trying to pick up an extra run off a misfield is another matter, though. It's unbelievable how many guys are run out off one — and that's only half the story. The guy still at the wicket feels bad about the run out and often gets out in the next few overs! That's poor cricket, because the team needs him to bat through and build up the score.

A couple more things: run a straight line and, when turning, don't swing wide and go 'via the Cape' as we say. Also, instead of doing a lap or two at training, do a few twenty-two yard sprints to sharpen up for running between wickets.

My advice to young players is to head out to a Test match and watch how the good players run between wickets. Ricky Ponting is a role model in this regard, and Michael Clarke and Mike Hussey are others who run quickly between wickets. Justin Langer and Matthew Hayden have a good understanding, too.

Lisa Sthalekar, a key member of the Australian women's team who weighs only 54 kilograms, shares my love of the single because she isn't big enough to bludgeon the ball to the boundary. She has plenty of shots but goes out for the long haul, an accumulator of runs who regards every ball as a possible single to keep the score ticking over.

WAZZA'S 1% FACTORS

BATTING

- Work as a pair while batting, discussing field placings, strong and weak fielders, the best scoring options and how the bowlers are trying to get you out.
- Congratulate your partner's good shots.
- Even if it means stopping the game between balls, calm your partner when necessary. Settle him down immediately if you see his concentration starting to waver.
- Switch off and relax between balls.
- Get a drink at the fall of a wicket or when you swap your helmet for a cap.

WATCH THE BOWLER

Always be aware of where the fast bowlers have set the field. Dennis Lillee would bowl outswingers to lots of slips and leave an inviting gap in front of the wicket on the off side. The old thimble and pea trick: big drive, snick, out. Let the swinging ball come to you and play it as late as possible.

With spin, it's easier and safer to play with the spin even if the ball is turning to crouching close-in fielders. Play forward only when you know you can smother the spin.

An experienced batsman can develop a type of sixth sense about a bowler's intentions from focusing on the latter stages of his approach. As he nears the bowling crease, there may be tell-tale signs of the sort of delivery he plans to bowl. For instance, if he intends to bowl a bouncer, he may accelerate, use his body more or carry an elbow slightly differently. Store away each bowler's characteristics. Of course, the bowler might play a mind game of his own. He may bowl a slower ball or go off a short run and then bowl a bouncer.

Greg Chappell used to say it was like having a television set in front of him. He'd concentrate on the bowler's head, shoulder and arm and finally his vision would shift to the wrist, from which he could judge what the bowler was attempting to do. A champion like Chappell could do that.

The golden rule is never to make a final judgment until the ball leaves the bowler's hand. That is when you make your first and last call. Second guessing can be dangerous, because if you've set yourself for a bouncer, what happens when you're faced with a yorker flying into the blockhole?

Beware of the breaks for lunch, tea and drinks if your mind is set on playing a long innings. How many times do you see a batsman lose a bit of concentration upon resuming and get out to a nick or a silly run out because he wasn't fully switched on? Such breaks mightn't have the potency of a Dennis Lillee or a Shane Warne delivery, but it's surprising how many times a team picks up a wicket after one.

WHAT'S FOR LUNCH?

What should a player have for lunch during the middle of an innings? It's an individual thing, of course. Sir Donald Bradman used to eat alone, ordering simply a few bread rolls, tinned fruit and weak tea. He'd break the rolls into small pieces and eat them dry washed down by the fruit. Four or five cups of milky tea and the Don was ready for his return to the field. Graham Thorpe, the England Test batsman who came to Sydney to play club cricket, would replace lost fluids with a sports drink and lunch on pasta or bananas, which are loaded with potassium.

DON'T BE JUST A BOUNDARY HITTER

One of the reasons budding champion Michael Clarke lost his spot in Australia's Test side was that he largely had become a boundary hitter. It happens to a lot of young players. They wait for the big shot, but with cricket coaches around the world poring over videos of such players, it doesn't take long to work them out. Captains set fields to cut off the boundaries, bowlers are told where to bowl, and suddenly the fours dry up. The boundary hitter becomes frustrated, plays a loose shot and is heading back to the pavilion.

Clarke burst onto the world cricket stage on a spectacular note. Australia was looking for an up-and-comer, and when he produced some blazing strokeplay to hit 151 against India in his Test debut at Bangalore, it looked as though they had found one. He followed up with another century against New Zealand in his first Test appearance in Australia.

Coinciding with a lift in the batting order to No 4, the runs dried up largely because Clarke had become a boundary hitter and switched-on captains were blocking the fours. When this happens, it's a matter of being patient, picking up the singles and pushing the ball into the gaps. Better to claw and scramble your way to an ugly sixty like Steve Waugh used to do than throw your wicket away to an impetuous shot when tied down early.

A long innings is all about control, and the more singles the better. Running between wickets is equally important, but that has never been a problem for Clarke. A couple of weeks after being dropped from the Test team in 2005 he had thirty-two singles to his name when he reached a one-day fifty against New Zealand. The lesson had obviously been learned.

For a while Michael Slater was a boundary hitter but the penny eventually dropped that you don't get any extra runs for slamming the ball into the fence so hard it bounces back. Ian Botham was a boundary hitter and Andrew Flintoff is another. Adam Gilchrist is one but he times the ball so well that, when he gets a bit of room, nobody can stop him. If the field is up, he goes right over the top. However, you will recall how Andrew Flintoff clipped Gilchrist's wings in the 2005 Ashes series by bowling round the wicket and cramping the Western Australian for space outside the off stump. And if he did go over the top, there was a sweeper waiting to block the four.

WAZZA TIP

WHEN YOU GET HIT

Justin Langer is the ultimate streetfighter. Time and again a fireball propelled by a fast bowler will thud into his body, doubling him up or sending him tumbling to the pitch. Inevitably he'll regain his feet and smile at the bowler. 'I'm okay,' he'll say. It's not a matter of being macho, it's part of a psychological game, because if the batsman shows pain the bowler's tail goes up. It's like playing footy and you crunch a bloke with a big tackle. If he gets up and smiles at you, it's going to be a difficult afternoon.

If you get hit, take your time facing up to the next ball, as it's going to be a yorker or a bouncer. Get your senses right so you know where you are. Talk to your partner and, if you're not feeling well, call for a drink. However, if you're still woozy, you must come off. It's not a sign of weakness.

I know what it's like to be battered and bruised by a fast bowler. When I was seventeen, I marched out to face Test quick Frank Misson in my first-grade debut for Sutherland with just an old Crockett bat and a thin pair of pads for protection. There were no helmets or thigh pads in those days and one ball after another thudded into my body.

WHEN A PLAYER HITS A SLUMP

It happens to everyone who picks up a cricket bat. Even Greg Chappell, who once tumbled to seven ducks in a season, three of them first-ballers, was beset by uncertainty at one point in his career.

In most cases the solution is simple, linked to one of the basics, but there are times when the problem is imaginary. Bob Simpson once told me he used to go through a mental checklist to see if the player really did have a technical worry.

I sit down with the player and ask him questions, eyeball to eyeball. He's got to be honest and this feedback provides an understanding of the bloke. Then I have a look at what he's doing. I check if his stance is correct, because that will determine how his feet are going to go. Is the head still or the bat being picked up late? I always look at the back shoulder, because if it's too far around he's going to hit with too much chest on. Young kids should have the eye and quick reflexes, but when a player gets a bit older there's a tendency for him to get squared up.

It's all about belief and trust between the player and his coach. When Michael Slater was dropped from the Australian team for the first time, he came down to Wagga, where I videoed him hitting balls from a bowling machine at an indoor centre. Then we sat down and went right back to square one. Michael was all over the place. His feet weren't in the correct position, the bat was coming in at a bit of an angle, and he was trying to hit the ball too hard. I think it was the result of what seemed to be seventeen million people telling him what to do.

I had to get inside his head. We sat and talked before I showed him an old tape of when he was at his top. 'That's what you used to be like,' I said. Then we looked at the footage of that day's video and Michael knew I was right. I did some throw-downs, getting him to come forward until he was back in the groove. Soon his feet were moving like the Michael Slater of old and his head was clear.

When you get to the level achieved by a Michael Slater, probably about ninety percent of the thing is in your head. It's a mental problem rather than a physical one. I think he had been distracted by a few things outside cricket, but eventually he was back scoring centuries for Australia.

Invariably the player having a bad trot will be getting one of the basics wrong. He might be worried sick about some little thing and get himself out. The absolute no-no for a player in a slump is to blaze away at everything in the hope of hitting his way out of it.

Sometimes it's a purely mental thing. A player might think he has a problem when one doesn't exist, and this should not be treated lightly. It happens quite often as a player rises through the ranks. You must be careful here. Don't overload him by telling him half a dozen different things, because there's only one red Kookaburra ball at a time coming down the pitch at him. In the split second it comes out of the bowler's hand, he must be concentrating solely on the ball, not on any technical problem.

Sometimes you've got to kid a bloke who's letting a minor problem upset his psyche. Errol Alcott, the long-serving Australian team physiotherapist, is said to keep a few white Smarties in his medical kit as a solution. One of Errol's magic white tablets can quickly effect a cure.

They all go through form slumps, even the great Viv Richards, who called in Dr Rudi Webster to sort out his woes by putting him under hypnosis when he started to struggle during the West Indies' tour of Australia in 1975/6. It worked, too. After a couple of treatments, Richards bounced back with a century in the Adelaide Test.

When Michael Clarke came into the Australian team, he was tempting fate when he said he hoped he would never be dropped. Don Bradman was briefly dumped (for a Brisbane doctor) after a single Test, and Keith Miller, Shane Warne, Steve Waugh, Ricky Ponting, Matthew Hayden and Justin Langer are among later victims of the selectorial axe. To a man, they fought their way back and returned better players.

WAZZA TIP

Luck can affect a performance in a negative or positive way. Too many players blame a poor performance on bad luck, while good players blame themselves and their efforts.

Brett Lee in full flight

4

FAST BOWLING

'Wouldn't it make more sense if I just got in the fridge?'

Qasim Omar, Pakistan batsman,
who needed six ice packs on wounds inflicted by Australian bowlers

A shiny red cricket ball in the hand of a fast bowler with anger in his heart can constitute a lethal weapon. Particularly when it comes whizzing at you from a distance of twenty yards at speeds approaching one hundred miles an hour.

It's part of the fast bowler's craft to flame-grill the batsman with bouncers, rib-ticklers and yorkers pitched at the batsman's toes — plus the odd verbal. Anybody who says they like to face genuinely fast bowling is either crazy or lying. Dennis Lillee was emphatic that he bowled bouncers to hurt the batsman and intimidate him, while Jeff Thomson once took this a step further. He declared that he enjoyed seeing blood on the pitch.

The fast bowler's job is the hardest in cricket, and until Shane Warne came along it was proved time and again that they really are the people who win Test matches and series. Fast bowling makes immense demands on a man's body. He needs strength in the legs to keep going and strength in his back, because this is where the effort will hit him most.

The textbook balance of Glenn McGrath

Who can a young bowler learn from? Watch good fast bowlers in action, men like Glenn McGrath, whose rhythm and balance when he gets to the crease in a sideways-on action is straight from the text book. Brett Lee is all about sheer pace and when he gets into full flight, he can be magnificent.

In terms of sheer style and smoothness, Michael Holding, the West Indian quick, was in a class of his own. Whispering Death, they called him. From a long, rhythmic run, Holding was as close to perfection as you could ever see. He would extend himself or hold a delivery back without any apparent change in his action. Holding was a wonderful sportsman, too, refusing to bowl on dodgy pitches when he played for Tasmania because he feared somebody could be seriously hurt. Not many fast bowlers would have done that.

TIP

'Performance is thirty percent physical and seventy percent mental. Because it is extremely powerful, the mind controls the body. It can help you achieve anything you are capable of achieving and sometimes more.'

Dennis Lillee

Malcolm Marshall, his West Indian colleague, had a perfect front-on action, while Dennis Lillee cut his pace and turned from a tearaway with long hair into a cunning technician. I'm still in awe of the magnificent flowing action of Alan Davidson which made him a supreme exponent of swing bowling in the fifties and early sixties. His left-arm deliveries brought him 186 Test wickets and at times he could be almost unplayable.

I'm not one of those coaches who think they know everything. My experience of fast bowling involves little more than putting myself in the line of fire, so I recruited Geoff Lawson, who has 180 Test wickets in his portfolio as the result of being one of the world's most dangerous pacemen. He had hauls of 8–112 in an innings against the Windies in

Adelaide and 7–81 (one of the remaining three was run out) against England at Lord's. He even had a knack of getting under the skin of the great Viv Richards, whom he once dismissed for a duck. On another occasion Lawson knocked Richards' West Indies cap off in a game at the SCG after bowling five maiden overs in succession to the champion. In 1984, West Indian captain Clive Lloyd described him as the fastest white bowler in the world, so when it comes to quick bowling, Henry knows his stuff.

ADVICE FOR COACHES OF ASPIRING FAST BOWLERS

Geoff Lawson says: 'Treat each bowler as an individual. Over the years in coaching I must have seen more than fifty thousand fast bowlers and I don't think I've seen two do it the same way. There's too much emphasis on bowling mechanics as far as kids are concerned. It should be about coaching bowlers to get people out, not about coaching them to get their left elbow in the right spot or their right shoulder in the right position.

'It's not just about mechanics. You've got to know the game, and coaches might say you don't have to have been a fast bowler to understand, but I'm telling you that you do. From the time you see a fourteen-year-old trying to bowl fast, it's a progression, a process. Think about what you're doing. Am I making this guy a better bowler? You add little things and be patient with what they do. When you see major errors, try to fix them but, whatever you do, let the kids enjoy what they're doing. It's not until they're eighteen or nineteen that you want them to be very good.

'When I'm coaching young fast bowlers, I tell them to keep their head as high as they can and keep it still. You look at the batsman rather than allowing the head to drop away. If you're landing it on the pitch and doing those two fundamental things, you're on the way.'

Geoff Lawson coaching

THE BASICS

A correct grip is crucial. To have control of the ball, hold it in the fingers, not the palm of the hand. Place your first and second fingers down the seam with the thumb underneath it and the two other fingers bent and resting comfortably on the side of the ball. The wrist is used to propel the ball, imparting the whip effect which gives zip to the ball off the pitch. According to Henry, ten percent of your pace comes from the wrist action. This grip allows the seam to rotate around the ball (top to bottom) in a continuous motion rather than from side to side. Thus the ball will land on the seam, making it more likely to grip the ground and move sideways, one way or the other.

The run-up must be right, otherwise there will be problems. Don't run further than is necessary, but do run long enough for you to build up speed stride by stride, gazing only at the spot where you want the ball to pitch. You peak three or four strides before delivery. Then hold the speed right through your action into the follow-through, making full use of height and body. It's all about rhythm and balance. Charging in can be a waste of valuable energy. You don't want to over-step your chosen point of delivery because, to avoid bowling a no-ball, your feet have to be planted in precisely the right spot.

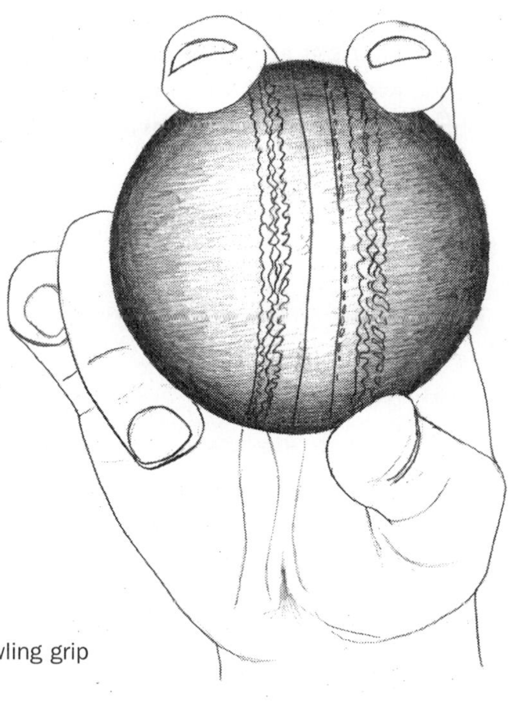

Fast bowling grip

SIDE-ON OR FRONT-ON?

There are two basic actions for fast bowling, the classic sideways-on action used by Dennis Lillee or the open, chest-on action practised by Malcolm Marshall. Feel comfortable about bowling either way and don't let any coach make you feel you have a second-rate action because it's front-on. The absolute no-no is to mix the two — shoulders pointed one way, hips another — because this is an open invitation to back problems. Apart from that, it hampers speed, rhythm and swing.

With the side-on method, you see an accelerating, menacing bowler, his head still as he presents the batter with a twist of the body, a thrust of the leading arm high into the air followed by the windmill action of the bowling arm rushing through at near maximum height before letting go the ball.

The chest-on fast bowler's back foot points down the pitch rather than being placed parallel with the bowling crease. Instead of gathering his body and rocking back, he runs through smoothly without much of a jump. The left shoulder goes up high, but the bowler looks at the batsman from inside the front arm. He never throws his shoulders into the sideways position but the follow-through is the same.

However, there are other ways to bowl fast. Jeff Thomson terrorised the world's finest batsmen in the seventies with a slinging action. He used to catapult the ball down after veering out on his arrival at the crease to make way for the right arm to sling the ball over from behind his back. His methods were technically excellent: feet square to the crease, shoulders right round, and a full, flowing arc.

WAZZA TIP

The follow-through is critical, and bowlers can suddenly find themselves bowling a yard or two faster by concentrating on it. The ball hits the wicketkeeper's gloves harder simply because the bowler has avoided losing half his speed by staying upright after releasing the ball.

I've often wondered if you could turn a javelin thrower into another Jeff Thomson, so when I saw a State javelin representative competing in a carnival at Gundagai I got him a cricket ball. Whoosh. The ball was a blur when he unleashed it, and for a moment I thought, 'I've got something here.' However, cricket held no appeal for him.

STRETCHING AND BOOT CARE

Geoff Lawson is adamant about two elements of the fast bowler's craft: stretching exercises and the proper choice and care of boots. 'When you're coaching fast bowlers at the higher level,' says Henry, 'you explain to potential State and international players that it's going to hurt. Pain is part of the process and stretching can help you avoid some of it.

'I was an enormous stretcher. Still am, as a matter of fact. What worked for me before a day's play was to get warm by running for ten minutes and then stretch thoroughly for thirty-five minutes out on the ground. Start really slowly, always keeping in mind that the hamstrings and lower back are incredibly important for a fast bowler. Start with the calves, quads and hammies and work your way through the sides, the lats, all the things you use when you're bowling. Do the shoulders and arms last because they tend to care for themselves. Look after the big muscle groups and all the things attached.

'When I was coming back from a back injury, I was given an Olympic sprinter's program and found it a most significant process. You walked, then jogged and, as everything got warm, you did the stretches gently and gradually.

'It's an absolute myth that today's fast bowlers are playing too much cricket. I've done some research that shows they bowl less in the nets and less in games than we ever did in the eighties, because we never missed a State or club game. Many of them are taking the soft option and don't do the hard work.

'With all our modern technology, recovery methods, dieticians, physios and fitness trainers, why are we getting more injuries than we used to? Why are we not producing more fast men who can bowl at 150 km an hour? There are lots of medium-fast bowlers but no new Brett Lees.

'Like a batsman's bat, the most important pieces of equipment for a fast bowler are his boots. When I talk to AIS players and the elite squads of NSW Cricket, we have a full session on the choice, care and maintenance of boots and feet. Where a fast bowler should cut holes in the toes, having the right length spikes in your boots, things like that.

WAZZA ON VERBALS

While ever this wonderful game of cricket is played, bowlers and fielders are going to try to psych out the batsman with a few well-chosen verbals. I have no problem with this providing nothing racist is said and it's not overdone. Fast bowlers are like a front-row forward in rugby league or a ruckman in the AFL. They've got to have a bit of pepper in them, don't they?

I don't mind one of my fast bowlers showing a bit of aggro if it gets him going, but he's got to be able to back it up. If he gets belted for three or four fours after winding up the batsman, he's lost the contest. Like when Yorkshire fast bowler Steve Kirby declared during a game against arch-rivals Lancashire in 2001, ' Umpire, I'm going round the wicket. Call the ambulance.' Chris Schofield hit the next ball for six. Indeed, a bit of sledging can serve to make the batsman doubly determined to succeed, which is why the Australians quickly gave up needling Brian Lara. It was like a red rag to a bull to the West Indian champion.

When a quick bowler fires a couple around your ears and comes down the wicket snarling at you, ignore him. Give him a smile and turn your back. Don't scuttle off as if there's urgent business to be done in another part of the crease. Brushing off the bowler can really get the anger running through his veins and then he's lost it. If things go further, the umpires should step in and say, 'Okay, that's enough.' Any more could be a turn-off to parents, who see thuggery in games like football and might be worried about letting their children play cricket.

Of course, there's a difference between sledging and banter. For instance, when Shane Warne, whose verbals can be as artful as his bowling, was bamboozling South African Justin Kemp in Perth in December 2005, he called down the wicket, 'I'm bowling leg-breaks,' adding, 'That's leg-breaks, Daryll.' It was a reference to another

South African, Daryll Cullinan, whose career as a Test batsman was wrecked by an inability to handle Warne's spin. That's banter at its best.

After discovering one time that Cullinan had sought psychological help in dealing with his bowling, Warne greeted his arrival at the crease with, 'Daryll, I've waited so long for this moment. I'm going to send you straight back to the leather couch.' Cullinan was out for a duck and missed the rest of the series.

Steve Waugh described this sort of baiting of a player with a suspect temperament as 'mental disintegration', a far cry from West Indian Malcolm Marshall's call to David Boon in a Test in Australia: 'Are you going to get out, or do I have to come around the wicket and kill you?'

When Michael Slater was playing well, he had a smile on his face that must have been annoying to some bowlers, and when Phil Jaques scored a spectacular 152 not out against Queensland in a one-dayer at the SCG, he seemed at times to be smiling at the bowler from under his helmet.

'Technology has come a long way, but some contemporary fast bowlers have no idea how to look after their footwear. I still see guys going out to open the bowling on first day wickets which are a bit moist wearing boots with the normal-length short spikes. You must have long spikes because if you can't stand up, you slip and can't bowl properly. You're slipping forward and bowling no-balls.

'I always wore custom-made high boots and taped both ankles before I bowled. The big and little toes, too, because they take most of the stress. The most painful injury I ever had was a bruised little toe because every time I bowled, I came over on it with all my body weight. It required needles and painkillers for some time.'

SWING BOWLING

I'm a country boy, so I'm not going to try to explain how the airflow and atmospheric resistance cause a cricket ball to swing, because I don't understand it. However, I do know that the ball will swing more consistently if one side is more shiny than the other, because the airflow on the rougher side and on the seam becomes disturbed. So, no matter how old the ball becomes, bowlers continue to shine the ball on their clothing. Fast bowlers expect to swing the new ball when it's still shiny and the seam firm and prominent, but the slower the ball is bowled, the more chance there can be of it swinging.

The most difficult ball for a batsman to play is the *outswinger*, which moves away to the slips before bouncing. The seam must be upright but pointed slightly towards first slip. Hold the ball loosely with the tips of the first two fingers close together on each side of the seam and the thumb underneath the seam. With the ball angled, the fingers will be slightly across the seam.

The shiny side of the ball must be on the outside, the side opposite to the way you want it to swing. When the ball is released, the seam must be vertical and angled in the direction of the intended swing. The position of the wrist is crucial. At the moment of delivery, ideally from the classical sideways-on action from close to the stumps, your bowling wrist cuts across the outside of the ball to help make it swing towards the off side. Make sure your arm follows through down the outside of your body, which is around the left hip for a right-arm bowler.

Outswinger

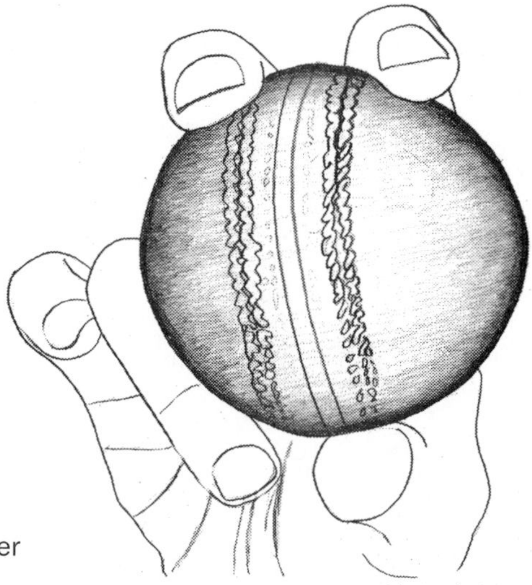

In-swinger

With *in-swing*, which ideally should swing late in flight towards the batsman before bouncing, place your first and second fingers along the seam, which should be pointing to fine leg. Again, it's important to keep the thumb on the seam underneath the ball. As the ball is released, the bowling wrist cuts down inside of the ball while the follow-through is down the inside of your body. Bob Simpson used to say that most right-handed bowlers fall away a little bit when they try to bowl the inswinger, so you could pick it.

Swing bowling once was a simple matter of holding the seam pointed to fine leg with the shiny side on the off side if you wanted to bowl an inswinger. For the outswinger, the seam pointed to third man with the shiny side reversed. However, all this changed when the Pakistanis Waqar Younis and Wasim Akram perfected the weapon of *reverse swing*. Their trademark became the deadly late reverse in-swinging yorker with the old ball. The offside of the ball is treated with sweat or spit and shined, with that side then becoming heavier and acting as a bias. The other side is allowed to deteriorate naturally, becoming rough and uneven, which causes friction through the air. So the ball swings to the shiny side — the opposite way to which it is supposed to — much later than with the traditional swinging delivery. Reverse swing is all about conning the batsman, and it caused no end of confusion among the Australian batters in the 2005 Ashes series.

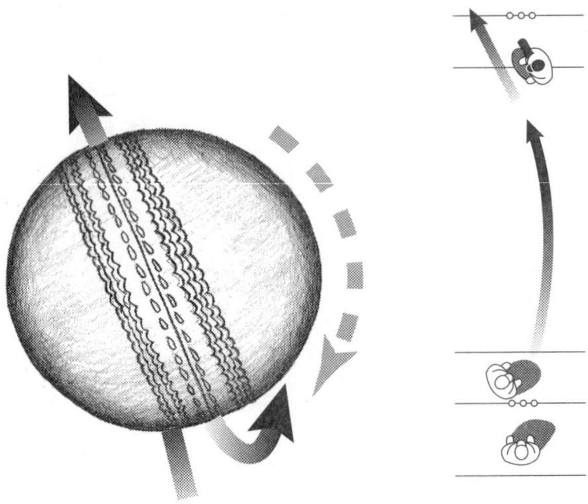

Normal

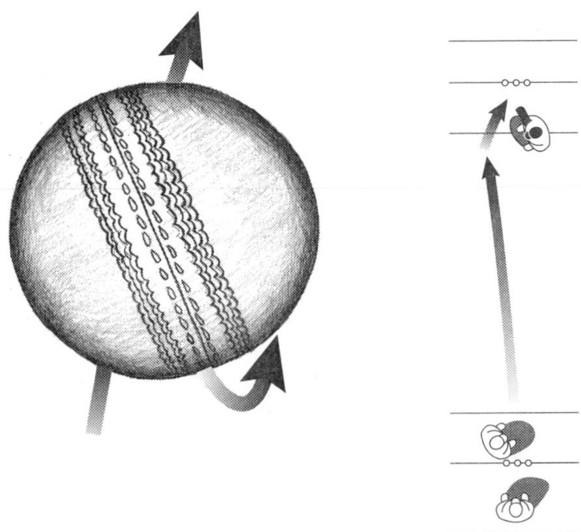

Reverse

There have been claims that the decline of the texture at times has been aided by thumbnails, bottle tops and dirt rubbed into the seam, and certainly these can have the effect of altering the flight of the ball. But reverse swing doesn't just depend on treating the ball, which is held in the palm and let out of the side of the hand when a switch is made to reverse swing. The bowling arm is lower in what is a supremely difficult art to perfect. As the ball will swing towards the shiny side, the batsman must watch the ball closely to pick the shiny half, and because it swings late you have to let the ball come to you. According to Dean Jones, you must play the ball as late as possible, while to avoid being yorked, batsmen like Matthew Hayden stand outside their crease in a bid to throw the bowler off his length.

WIND BALL

A tennis ball carefully shaved so one side is completely bereft of fuzz has played a big part in the development of a wave of West Indian bowlers of lightning pace and batsmen and fieldsmen of extraordinary reflexes.

It's used in a game called 'wind ball', played on the water's edge of the sandy Caribbean beaches. The bowlers, who each have their own ball, time their run-up to coincide with the gentle run-out of the waves. When it hits the wet but firm sand in front of the batsman, the shaven projectile generates frightening pace and erratic bounce. Throwing is allowed and there's a cordon of four or five slips. From Garry Sobers down, all the West Indian heroes developed their skills playing this form of beach cricket.

HANDLING THE BOUNCER

Bouncers are a test of a batsman's courage, with the threat of physical danger often prompting impotent shots. If the red sphere is exploding like a rocket from the pitch and rearing at your head, you must keep your eye on the ball and not freeze.

If you're an early order batsman, you can expect more than the odd bouncer and you have two options: attack it or avoid it. If you decide on the latter course of action, either duck or stay upright and sway out of the line of the delivery, keeping your eye on the ball as long as possible. Never turn the head away. When avoiding the ball in the upright position, be sure that your hands stay low and out of the line of the ball. It only has to brush your gloves and there's the danger of a catch. If you duck low, don't take your eye off the ball.

Always wear a helmet for safety when facing the physical and mental onslaught of pace bowlers. It will be like waving the proverbial red rag at a bull if you don't. Forget about Viv Richards not wearing a helmet, because you are hardly likely to be in the class of the famous West Indian. Admittedly Richards never had to bat against his venomous countrymen, but India's Sunil Gavaskar did for years, and was hit only once. Short in stature, his lack of height helped him negotiate countless fast bowlers, especially those from the West Indies, against whom he scored a record thirteen centuries. He never wore a helmet, just a little plastic scull cap under his floppy white sunhat. His friend, the Nawab of Pataudi, once explained, 'You have to realise how perfectly positioned are Sunil's feet — and hence his bat — whenever he plays a stroke. That is why he never gets hit by bouncers. If your feet are in the correct position, so is your head.'

Myself, I serve a tennis ball from halfway down the pitch on a hard surface so it flies at the batsman head high. Wearing pads, gloves and helmet, he practises ducking and weaving like a boxer, keeping his eye on the ball at all times. This will help him cope with the bouncing ball.

When Michael Slater was opening for Australia, he went into the nets padded up and helmeted to face colleagues who stood halfway down the pitch and hurled bouncers at his head with a real cricket ball. However, be warned that this can be a dangerous form of practice unless you have confidence in the thrower.

If you've been rattled by a bouncer, clear your mind before the next ball. There could be a fast yorker or a slower ball coming that catches you unawares. Be prepared for anything. Andy Roberts, the West Indian fast bowler, had two bouncers, one distinctly slower than the other but bowled with an almost identical action. There was little clue how high or quickly the ball would bounce, and the batsman often ducked into it.

Bob Simpson was a happy hooker when he came into first-class cricket at the age of sixteen, but after becoming an opening batsman he decided the shot was too risky. He took it from his repertoire and worked hard on a safer, more productive method of dealing with the short ball.

BRADMAN ON PLAYING FAST BOWLING

Lunching with Sir Donald Bradman one unforgettable day when I was in Adelaide doing a spot of coaching with the Australian Under 19s, I was cheeky enough to ask for a few tips on playing the fastest of bowling. He was happy to oblige.

Sir Donald said: 'My first movement was to move my rear foot slightly back and across simultaneously with lifting the bat. At the instant the ball left the bowler's hand, the end of my blade would be approximately the height of the bails and my back foot would be covering middle stump. From that initial movement, it was easy to continue the back movement to a short-pitched ball or to reverse it and come forward to, say, a half volley.

'Sometimes, when well set, I might have varied this, especially against a slow bowler if I was seeking to drive, but then one often did unorthodox things when the conditions were favourable and one was set.

'Against Harold Larwood, I often deliberately moved, sometimes to leg, sometimes to off, just to try to confuse him and try to put him off his direction of the body. I have seen a shot of me making a pull shot which looks more like a Pete Sampras serve.'

5

SPIN BOWLING

Nothing excites me more than watching a wrist-spinner like Shane Warne bowling to a batsman who can use his feet. When Warne is bowling, I can't leave the television set. You can fall asleep when the military mediums are operating, but not the spinners. Guys can be bowling leggies, offies, left-arm orthodox and Chinamen. There are other deliveries such as the topspinner, flipper, doosra and slider. Not to mention the 'nude ball' that has nothing on it.

If you want to be a spinner, learn to spin the ball hard before you do anything else. I like to see kids spinning a ball from hand to hand or spinning an apple or an orange before they eat it. Their hands are soft, and spinning away like this strengthens them. To me, a spinner is a bit like a pianist, so when I see a young spinner, the first thing I look at is their hands. The really good spinners have long fingers, particularly those who bowl off-spin.

The off-spinner needs long fingers with which to grip the ball and put a genuine rip on it, while leg-spinners like Warne and Stuart MacGill come from the back of the hand, using their fingers to produce a variety of problems for the batsmen.

A good spinner is able to deceive the batsman in flight, which is very important, and if the wicket turns a bit the wrist-spinner must be accurate, which is a hard art to master. It's like bowling into a channel the way Glenn McGrath does. What I like about the good leg-spinner is that he has so many strings to his bow. For instance, Warne has the big turner, the little turner, the flipper, the slider, the topspinner and the wrong 'un, which disappeared for a while but resurfaced in 2005.

My advice to a budding spinner? Rip it as hard as you can, really spin the ball and bowl lots and lots of overs in the nets to develop the accuracy you need. If there isn't a batsman available, put something on the ground at which you can bowl. They reckon the great Bill O'Reilly would put a two shilling coin on the pitch at the SCG nets and Richie Benaud used a handkerchief as a target.

Richie now advises to make the mark with a white shoe cleaner that will wash off when the curator later waters the pitch. To find the exact spot, go to the batting crease with a bat and work out the spot where you as a batsman would least like a leg break to land. That's where to put the mark. From the time you run in to bowl to a batsman, the eyes must be fixed on the exact spot on the pitch where you want the ball to land. Not the batsman's feet, the base of the stumps, nor anywhere else.

Clarrie Grimmett, the legendary Australian leg-spinner who always bowled with his cap on to hide his baldy head, trained a dog to retrieve the ball when he spent lonely hours bowling practice balls.

LEG SPIN

Over-the-wrist spin is a world of fascinating variations. The three classical weapons are the leg break, googly and flipper. If bowled to a right-handed batsman, the *leg break* is the bread-and-butter ball, moving from the leg to off after pitching if bowled to a right-handed batsman. The ball is gripped with the third finger down the seam. As the ball is released, the wrist is turned sharply and the back of the hand faces the bowler.

The *googly*, also known as a *wrong 'un*, looks like a leg break but spins in the opposite direction. The only difference comes at the point of release, where the back of the hand is facing the ground. Ian Salisbury, the England Test leggie who played for University of NSW, had two wrong 'uns, an obvious one that he bowled first up and a cleverly disguised variation. Included among Ian's Test scalps were Javed Miandad

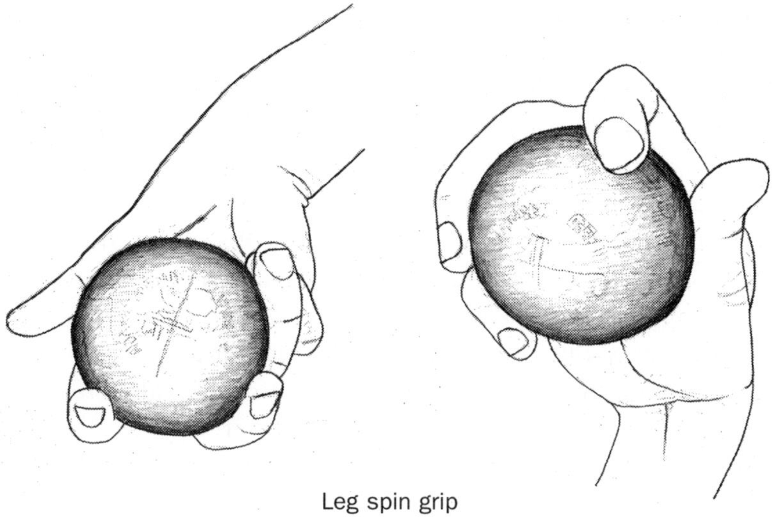

Leg spin grip

and Sachin Tendulkar, so he knew what he was about. The players say that Stuart MacGill's wrong 'un is better disguised than that of Shane Warne, but I'd settle for either of them.

The *flipper*, which has been described as a grenade dressed up as a gift, arrives before the batsman expects it. With the back of the hand facing the heavens, the ball is squeezed out between the tips of the fingers and thumb. Upon pitching, it skids low and fast with back-spin, making it prime LBW material. Clarrie Grimmett had a flipper and so did Richie

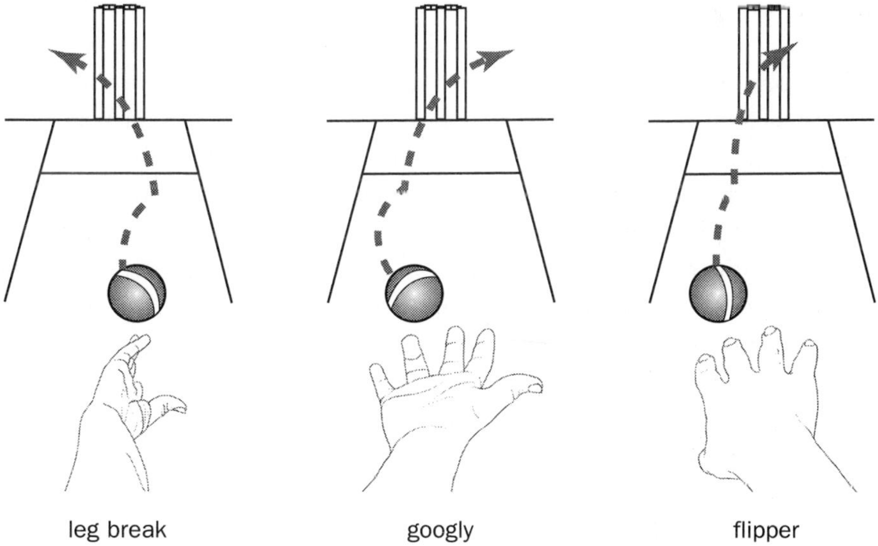

Benaud. Grimmett experimented with it for twelve years before he dared use it in a first-class game, while Benaud needed four years to perfect it. Richie did hours and hours of practice, especially to strengthen the ligaments and tendons in the hand because the ball was flipped from underneath the wrist rather than over the top and came from a slightly different arm action. The flipper puts a great strain on the ligaments, tendons and muscles and should not be attempted by young bowlers until their bodies are strong. Perfect the leg break first and this itself will take at least four years.

It would be foolish to be too pragmatic about the various grips, though. There is a famous story about a country boy called Bill O'Reilly being told by officials to change his grip after the veteran Test leg-spinner Arthur Mailey stated adamantly that no player who held a ball like that could take first-class wickets. Thankfully O'Reilly, the man nominated by Bradman as the best bowler he ever faced, refused to take heed. Mailey, by the way, is said to have carried a billiard ball in his pocket, twisting it to make his tremendously strong fingers even stronger whenever he had a spare moment.

SHANE WARNE'S ARMOURY

Shane Warne is a prodigious spinner of the ball, and the volume of spin imparted to his leg break is such that the ball dips into the right hander late in flight before gripping the surface. The most perfect example of that lethal dip is Warne's supernatural delivery to Englishman Mike Gatting at Old Trafford in 1993 — still unchallenged as the 'ball of the century'. In Gatting's mind, it drifted in, fizzed from somewhere near the square-leg umpire's toecaps, and somehow skittled his off stump.

According to Richie Benaud, Warne's wrist is in the perfect position for a bowler of his type. Apart from the leg break, wrong 'un and flipper, Warne has the topspinner, zooter and slider at his command, along with variations in wrist position, the height of his arm and whether he attacks from round the wicket or not. He can make the ball drift and drop, often savagely. Although capable of prodigious turn, Warne regulates the amount of spin he imparts. He uses the big ripper sparingly, and adds top- or side-spin for further variety. And wait, there's more: a slower one with more bounce.

His *top spinner* goes straight through but dips more in the air and then jumps off the pitch. It's released from out of the back of the hand midway between the release for the googly and leg break. The *zooter*

The powerful follow-through of Shane Warne

behaves similarly but looks more like a leg break when it leaves the hand. The *slider*, a variation of the zooter, goes straight on like the flipper but is bowled at a slower pace.

On a flat pitch Warne can bowl nice and tight, with the drift on his leg break so pronounced that it keeps the batsman pinned to the crease. The bounce he gets from his topspinner has a similar effect. Only the most daring dance down the wicket to him.

Technically, Warne is magnificent. After a slow, deliberate walk back, his back leg drive is the key to achieving energy on the ball. The perfect timing of shoulder rotation ensures excellent ball flight and pace.

Shane has exceptionally strong hands and fingers, and they say that from where the bowler's umpire stands you can hear the ball fizzing out of his hand and displacing the air as it spins down the pitch.

OFF-SPIN

It is generally agreed that the greatest of the off-spinners have been Jim Laker of England, Lance Gibbs of the West Indies and the Sri Lankan Muttiah Muralitharan. The batsman at the non-striker's end heard the ball hum with spin as it left Laker's hand, with the Englishman mixing control and intelligence with this attribute. Laker has an unshakable niche in cricketing lore for his feat of snaring nineteen wickets against Australia in the Old Trafford Test of 1956. Gibbs, a spindly chap with very long fingers, captured 309 Test wickets for the Windies.

Once asked how one might discover a top-class off-spinner, Laker said he would seek a youth of eighteen or nineteen, about 5 ft 10 in (175 cm) in height with long, strong fingers, suppleness of wrist, a good basic action and the patience to serve a five-year apprenticeship. First, he must learn to bowl a reasonable line and length and spin the ball more than most. Then come the intricacies of flight and how to bowl on differing pitches and to control the amount of spin. Under no circumstance should he play limited-over cricket at a good level until he's ready for it.

When bowling off-spin, grip the ball tightly between the top joints of the first and second fingers with the seam virtually at right angles to them. The idea is to spin the ball hard with the index finger and some help from the middle finger, rotating the hand and ball in a clockwise direction.

Cricket is a sideways game, so the delivery action to bowl off-spin is a sideways one like a cartwheel, with the front arm high and the delivery stride fairly short. The most productive line for an off-spinner is at the off stump or just outside. Loop in flight is a must, with the ball coming out over the top of the index finger. The fingers cut less across the ball and more through it.

One off-spin weapon is the *arm ball*. The batsman expects an off-break because he sees the pretence of off-spin but a last-second deception with the fingers makes the ball drift away to slip. Instead of placing the index finger across the seam, place it alongside. The batter can still see the off-spin grip from his end, but you let the ball straight out without cocking the wrist or spinning the ball. When you bowl the arm ball to drift away, have the shiny side of the ball facing leg, dip into your normal sideways action without the hard spin of the fingers, and follow through across the body.

Another weapon is the *doosra*. Muttiah Muralitharan, the Sri Lankan whose extravagant off-breaks with a helicopter wrist action have brought him phenomenal success, needed a new delivery to keep the batsman guessing. The answer was the doosra, a word used in Hindu and Urdu which means 'other one'. Instead of spinning into the right-hand batter, with the change in action cleverly disguised it spins away from him. The bowler employs the same grip as for an off-break but uses three fingers to spin the ball instead of two. To bowl the doosra, the back of the hand faces the batsman, the wrist rotates towards him and the ball spins from the back of the hand in the opposite direction. After Muralitharan used the doosra to sink England at home in 2003, there were allegations of throwing, and the authorities ruled that he unduly bent his arm in delivering his 'other one'. However, after a brief ban he was back bowling it.

A final point: when a top-class batter is well set, the finger-spinner can set his field to a pattern and force the batsman to hit the ball into a defensive web. Bowl at the right-hander's middle and leg stump, place six fielders on the leg side, with three in the inner ring saving the single and three on the boundary.

WHY SO FEW LEFT-ARM WRIST SPINNERS?

Johnny Martin, whose googly is known for some reason in cricketing parlance as a Chinaman, was saluted by fellow purveyors of left-handed leg breaks when he captured the wickets of Rohan Kanhai, Frank Worrell and Garry Sobers in the space of four balls in his Test debut against the West Indies in 1960/61. There is no higher-risk brand of spin bowling than unorthodox left-arm, which is great if it works but prone to go expensively wrong if it doesn't.

David Sincock was another bowler of this style who spun the ball like a top, but there have been few others to play Test cricket for Australia. Brad Hogg is the latest, while Michael Bevan took wickets in Tests with left-arm wrist-spin, but of course he was primarily a batsman. David Freedman came close, playing for Australia A and once capturing eight wickets in an innings for NSW against the West Indies in Newcastle. I asked 'Freddie' about the shortage of such left-arm wrist spinners: 'The secrets are hard work and having a thick skin. You can't just roll the ball out, you've got to really spin it, give it a good rip. Right-arm wrist spinners are going away from the bat, so the slips are always in play, but if the left-hander bowls a bad ball, it's heading across to the batsman's leg side. So you're going to have more bad days than good days. A lot of young left-handers see Shane Warne on TV and want to try wrist spin, but they soon realise it's a pretty hard road to hoe and go back to bowling quicks.'

When he is at work, Freedman, a High Performance coach with Cricket NSW, insists that youngsters try to spin the ball fiercely. If they can achieve this crucial ingredient, sheer hard work will bring a degree of control. When he was taking first class wickets, Freddie had a couple of stock balls turning in to the right-hander with various degrees of spin. Sometimes there was a touch of over-spin and he used the crease to add further deception. He was happy with his Chinaman but never had a great flipper. He didn't have the variation of Shane Warne and Stuart MacGill, but neither did any other left-hand wrist spinner.

Freedman says it's helpful for a wrist spinner to operate in partnership with a colleague bowling in miserly fashion: 'I was blessed to have Greg Matthews bowling his off-spin at the other end in most of my matches for NSW. He'd tie them down, tempting the batsman to play a few shots against me. I can thank Greg's accuracy for a lot of my wickets.'

SETTING THE FIELD

To bowl spin against a top-class batsman, a bowler must set his field with the preciseness and cunning of a chess grandmaster. Sometimes you'll see the fieldsman move less than a metre and make a mark on the turf to ensure he's on the very spot required by his captain or the bowler. Watch Shane Warne or Stuart MacGill make a last minute check of the field before presenting the ball to the batsman.

Often a bowler will leave an inviting gap in the field to challenge a batsman to take a chance and hit the ball through it. In the thirties Bradman had a famous shot to long-on, and when he came to bat on a sticky wicket in the Lord's Test in 1934, English spinner Hedley Verity took the fieldsman away from long-on to leave a gap there. However, to take advantage of this, Bradman would have to hit across the spin, a most dangerous thing to do in such conditions. For fifteen minutes the Australian kept looking towards the gap but, with skipper Bill Woodfull warning him to be careful, he resisted the temptation. Then came a delivery from Verity that the great man could no longer ignore. Bradman struck at the ball, which found the bat's edge, flew up and was caught behind the wicket. It was a defining moment of a game that Australia lost by an innings.

KEEP IT SIMPLE

It's dumb cricket to bowl too many types of delivery in an over. Keep it down to two, or three at the most. Any more than that and you're playing with fire. You lose your line and length and, because you can't take a wicket with every ball, you get hit.

If you're bowling to a bloke and he can't get you away, why change your pattern? I get *very* annoyed when one of my spinners bowls five dot balls, then does something different with the last and it goes for four. He had the batsman pegged down and now the momentum has changed. Of course, I'm not against buying a wicket if you've got enough runs and a guy like Stuart MacGill in your side. He spins the ball a bit more than Shane Warne and loves the batsman to go after him.

But in most cases it pays to stick with what is working. You might have a seam bowler bowling a good outswinger and three slips and two gullies waiting for a nick. Why change? Stick to the game plan.

PLAYING SPIN

Some players watch the ball coming out of the spinner's hand, trying to fathom if it's a wrong 'un or a big leg break, while others read it off the pitch, which is harder. Neil Harvey was sheer magic when it came to dancing down the wicket to a spinner, and we can only dream of him taking on Warne. When asked how he would play the Victorian, Harvey is said to have replied, 'The ball wouldn't hit the pitch.' In other words, he'd be down the track like a bull terrier after a live kill to nullify the spin. That's how quick he was. Of course, when Warne sees that happening, he's going to drop the ball a little bit shorter and the fun begins. Allan Border at his peak was another exceptional player of spin.

6

WICKETKEEPING

According to Steve Waugh, the wicketkeeper is the heartbeat of a team, the one that sets standards for the rest of the side with his energy and enthusiasm. On the other hand, Rod Marsh claims that keeping wickets is for the adventurous, those who bore easily and, on reflection, those with just a touch of stupidity.

Bob Simpson, a font of cricketing wisdom, has always said that the last person you want to change in any team is the wicketkeeper. He's the captain's second pair of eyes, and although he must attack the half-chance he needs the patience to wait for it. In the old days, wicketkeepers didn't have to bat, but now it's rare to find a Test team in which the keeper bats lower than seven or eight.

I love watching a nice, neat wicketkeeper with good balance and footwork and soft hands. These days he's more of an all-rounder because the days of a keeper doing his best at No 11 have long gone. Adam Gilchrist is never going to go down as the greatest keeper of all time because he misses too many balls, but without doubt he is the finest

TIP

Don't be frightened to speak up. Ian Healy says: 'To me, a noisy wicketkeeper is much more effective than a quiet one. The keeper's job is to be in the thick of things. I always tried to be chirpy, encouraging and enthusiastic.'

keeper-batsman the game has seen. The wicketkeeper also has to be the fittest man in the team because he must be a livewire who is moving all the time.

Few people know as much about wicketkeeping as Alan Campbell, back-up to Steve Rixon as NSW keeper for ten years and now manager of Cricket NSW's High Performance coaching unit. In a most eloquent manner, he was happy to share his knowledge of what makes a top class gloveman tick: 'Wicketkeeping is all about agility and footwork. I look for people who are like the halfback in rugby — nimble, sharp and a quick mover. A person who has the ability to watch the ball into the hands, which not everybody can do. The biggest fault I see among budding keepers in Australia is footwork. They might have great hands, but they don't move their feet to cover the line of the ball properly.'

THE STANCE

Wearing a cap or floppy hat to protect your eyes from the glare, crouch just outside the line of the off stump. For fast bowlers, stand far enough back to catch the ball as it stops rising. It's the keeper who must dictate where he stands, how close to the stumps and where the slips must take station, according to the variables of pitch, bowler and ball. Keeping wickets is all about footwork, timing and rhythm backed by lots of stretching to stay supple. Balance is everything.

Balancing on the balls of the feet, the wicketkeeper squats with his weight evenly distributed so he can move quickly in any direction. The stance must be comfortable and provide a clear view of the bowler's hand through the run-up and delivery.

The superbly balanced stance of Brad Haddin

TAKING THE BALL

Footwork and glovework go together like Jack and Daniels, and the ball must always be watched right into your gloves. Never, ever point your fingers at the ball. Point them down for takes below the chest and up for takes above the chest, and use both hands whenever possible. As you take the ball, give with your hands, arm and body to avoid sore hands and prevent the ball from bouncing out. Let the ball come to you and never snatch at it. Keep your head and eyes over it as much as possible.

Let the ball come to you

STANDING BACK

With a quick bowler, the ball will whip through fast and hard with plenty of bounce, so you should be far enough back to catch the ball as it stops rising. Move quickly into position behind the ball to try to take it on the side of your body closest to the stumps. Your hands, arms and body should give with the ball as it falls into your gloves. Move quickly to the stumps to be ready to run out the batsman or a take a return from a fielder.

THE DIVING CATCH

The rule is that you try to catch everything in both gloves. If the ball is flying low and hard to your right, you go with two hands initially. If the ball is too far away, then stretch out the right hand to catch it, supporting the body with your left hand. If it's higher to your right, then generally speaking, use your feet to cover the ground.

Catch the ball as late as possible, remembering Bob Simpson's advice to catch it when it's behind the line of your body. Thus you give yourself a few extra seconds to sight the snick.

When do you go for the diving catch and when do you leave it to first slip? This is where the keeper is boss, because he determines where first slip stands. He's the one who knows his extension, how far he can go and how quickly he can cover ground. If necessary, the keeper can tell the first slip to go a little bit wider. 'Never hesitate,' is Adam Gilchrist's motto when the 50-50 ball enters the airspace between the pair.

With leg-side diving catches, obviously the keeper has more ground to cover, so he must move his feet first. If it's a deflection that's going wider, then you might have to dive. It can be a low catch from a glance or a high one when the batsman tries to hook a bouncer and leaves the keeper with a one-handed, left-handed catch. What we don't want to see is young people diving without using their feet to balls that aren't that wide of the leg stump.

STANDING UP

According to Alan Campbell, a wicketkeeper must love standing up to the stumps. If he's fearful of it, he's not in the game. The key to this crucial phase is to relax, keep the head and shoulders forward in a nice stance, and come up as the ball comes up. If you come up too quickly, you've got to go down again and this creates problems. Caress the ball into your gloves, but do it slowly so you're not snatching at it.

Campbell admits that as a youngster he used to flinch a bit when the batsman would go back to cut a ball, but got the technique right with the help of his mother's Hills Hoist clothesline in the back yard. Alan would toss a ball up into it and wait for it to bounce down towards his face. Sometimes it would hit part of the Hills Hoist, and he made himself keep his eye on the ball without turning his head.

It's a bit like the man on the trapeze. There's a certain element of fear while standing up on the stumps when the ball is kicking up off a length. You can get hit in the eye, the teeth or the face, but once you learn the technique it's unlikely this will happen. There's a specific technique for standing over the stumps on turning wickets. When a spinner is bowling, the keeper should stand as close to the off stump as is comfortable. It's quicker for stumping and you can see more easily around a batsman to sight a ball before it goes down the leg side. However, some keepers prefer to stand a little deeper as it gives a trifle more time to sight the ball.

Standing up, some keepers rest their hands on the ground between their legs, while others await the ball with their gloves off the ground. Whatever helps their balance. The feet are perhaps shoulder width apart. When taking a basic ball outside the off stump while standing up, move from the hips and knees while taking the ball. The hardest balls to take are the yorker and the half volley to the batsman, with much practice needed taking such deliveries.

Young guys standing up to the stumps often fumble or miss the ball because they think the batter is going to hit it, so the mind-set they should develop is that the bowler is bowling to them. ('He's bowling to me, he's bowling to me.') Once you get that in your brain, you're more prepared to take all the bullets. Even if it's an easy full toss, stay switched on.

LEG-SIDE DELIVERIES

It's easier when a pace bowler slips one down the leg side because you have more time to sight the ball. As soon as you pick up the angle, take off so you have plenty of time to glove the ball.

It's much harder to take a leg-side delivery when standing up to a spinner because you're so much closer to the ball. The blind spot is larger, making it all about anticipation, intuition and practice. If it's short of a length, you can actually sight the ball, so hands and feet go simultaneously as you step across to the leg side. Generally your head is the last thing that moves, because you want as much information from the ball as possible.

If the ball is fuller, you don't actually see where it lands because of the batsman's body. Try to make certain that your hands get across to cover the ball as quickly as possible.

Footwork and speed of reaction are crucial. Providing there's plenty of room to move, the more you can practice in a net behind a spinner the better.

STUMPING

When a stumping is on, the important thing is not to grab at the ball in your anxiety to get it back to the stumps. You must be in a position to reach them in one movement, using your arms and hands in the action to remove the bails.

All stumpings are different. Stumping off a medium pacer is generally slightly easier because the ball hits the gloves a little harder. Generally the medium pacer lands the ball in areas you can see, and you'll know how fast it's coming, where it's going and how high it's going to bounce. It's a matter of timing, coming up with the ball, gloving it softly and bringing it back to the stumps.

Stumping to a Shane Warne or Stuart MacGill spinning the ball hard when it's bouncing and turning, say at the Sydney Cricket Ground, is much more difficult. You need to 'give' with the ball a little bit longer. If it's a leg-spinner where the ball is pitching middle and leg and bouncing high to your right, it's important that you 'give' with the ball and open the right hip up so you can take the ball in line and past your body. It's the same with the off-spinner going down leg side. Open the left hip up to allow the ball to come past your body.

The difficult ones from a medium pacer are the balls sliding into the pads off a good length. The easy balls are ones that are full like a half volley. People think they're difficult but they're actually easier, particularly down leg side. People see a leg side stumping and say, 'That's brilliant.' Actually the ball hits your gloves fairly hard and sinks in, and the batsman has generally fallen over or lost balance, so you've got a bit more time to get back to the stumps.

For wider deliveries, most keepers move their whole body, led by knees and hips. Don't become preoccupied about a stumping when the batsman heads down the track. After all, it might be a catch, so just concentrate on taking the ball.

Here's an ideal way to sharpen your stumping method or general takes while standing up. Go into a net, which is a perfect place for a keeper to practise, and get a batsman to charge down the pitch, hitting some balls and deliberately missing others. Another thing is to put objects like little cones, bits of cloth or a stump on a length where the ball is going to land. These can distract you by causing the ball to bounce awkwardly or sharply in a different direction.

Practising with his Kent and England colleague Derek Underwood, Test keeper Alan Knott used to take his stance on the length that

Underwood wanted to bowl at with his brisk spinners. When Knott put his gloves down, they would become Underwood's target. He'd bowl to those gloves on the full. What it did for Knott was that it kept him down in his crouch, because when the ball is coming at you on the full you're supposed to stay in that position. It taught Knott to stay down, maintain his balance and give with the ball. It was dangerous but the danger was overcome with continual practice of that method and not flinching or turning his head or trying to avoid the ball.

PROTECTING YOUR HANDS

Doug Ford, the former NSW wicketkeeper, used to tape each joint of each finger and thumb before taking the field, and as a result he has hands that would not be out of place on a Las Vegas card dealer. In contrast, Brad Haddin, the keeper groomed to succeed Adam Gilchrist behind the stumps for Australia, simply tapes the index and little fingers. The golden rule is that if you play or practice with an injury, tape it.

Alan Campbell says: 'You have to be careful at pre-season training when your hands are soft and the practice balls are hard. Next thing you've got idiots throwing rock balls at you at 100 miles an hour. I used to wear two pairs of inners to prevent injury.'

PRACTICE METHODS

Throughout his career, Ian Healy, named as the keeper in Australia's Team of the Twentieth Century, threw a golf ball against a wall to sharpen his technique. He would bounce it before the wall so it would come back on the full, and he could practise sideways movement as well as balance and rhythm as he watched it into the inner gloves he was wearing. You've got to have great hands to catch a golf ball. A tennis ball, too.

However, be careful of windows and open doors. Growing up at Inverell, Alan Campbell used to throw a golf ball as hard as he could into the wall of his house until the day one took an awkward bounce, flew through the open front door and smashed his mother's treasured Queen Elizabeth Royal Doulton plate.

As a keeper's feet must move quickly, Campbell says skipping can sharpen his agility, as can a game like squash in which a player moves laterally at speed. Anything that involves leg-strengthening and feet sharpness. Climbing one step up and one step back. Draw a line on the ground and jump two feet across and two feet back as many times as you can. Run up and down the wicket. Lots of stretching, too.

DON'T RUSH IT

Ian Healy warns budding wicketkeepers that being in their crouch for too long can lead to back and knee problems. The mind and body must be relaxed, the gloves soft and the feet moving in the correct manner. Position yourself outside the off stump so the batsman can't obscure your view.

Before every ball from a slow bowler, Healy used to say to himself, 'Watch the ball ... move ... stay down.' He waited for the ball, never grabbing for it, eyes on it and feet moving into position. The gloves stayed relaxed to give with the ball, and in it went cleanly.

Alan Campbell says: 'Rise as the ball rises and that'll give you the timing of gloving the ball. The young wicketkeeper often comes up and is in a catching position too early. He has to go back down and therefore the timing is out and he snatches at the ball. It's a matter of the ball finding the gloves rather than the gloves pushing and going towards the ball.'

WATCH THOSE PRESSURE POINTS

A long day keeping wickets can be tough on the feet, so Alan Campbell used to have two pairs of shoes, each with spikes in different positions. If he wore the same shoes, there would be pain from the pressure point where the spikes were, which could affect his concentration. Change your shoes at lunch and tea. Obviously keeper's boots have more spikes on the front of the foot because you spend so much time on your toes.

WAZZA'S 1% FACTORS

Alan Knott, who rarely fumbled a ball when he kept wickets for England in the seventies, caught the eye with his flamboyant manner and red gloves. He also had his shirts specially made with longer sleeves and tails so as not to interfere with his movement.

KEEPING WARM ON A COLD DAY

Before taking the field, fill a sink with hot water and soak your hands in it so they're nice and warm before slipping on the inner gloves.

ARE WICKETKEEPERS BORN OR MADE?

Providing a player has the ability to sight and catch the ball, he can develop into a worthwhile keeper with intense training in speed, agility and footwork, says Alan Campbell. After all, young people can be trained to do triple pirouettes and awesome dives off the high tower. Not only does Campbell disagree with the old adage that wicketkeepers are born not made, he doesn't think they can be 'too tall'. He points to Adam Gilchrist, who stands 186 cm.

7

FIELDING

With so much first-class cricket being played on flat, lifeless wickets, bowlers, with the support of aggressive fielding, must force the batsmen to make mistakes by drying up the scoreboard. The fielder doesn't have to touch the ball to add to the pressure. By thinking about the game, he can cut off an angle that denies the batsman a single.

People like the freakish South African Jonty Rhodes have turned it into an art form. These days the fielders must take the field with an aggressive, attacking attitude. They must enjoy it and want every ball to come to them. It's more than simply taking the catches — you're cutting off the fours and turning prospective twos and threes into ones and two. With so much one-day cricket being played, there's no place for a sloppy fielder.

Spectacular fielding is nothing new, of course. In the fifties, South Africa's Colin Bland was dynamic in the covers, while Neil Harvey, Clive Lloyd and Viv Richards were also famed for their fielding. Richards once effected three run-outs in a World Cup final at Lord's. There have always been dashers in the field, but nowhere near as many as there are today. The top sides simply do not have a bad fieldsman.

My advice to any young cricketer is to treat fielding just as importantly as batting or bowling. Nobody wants to be the player who drops an early catch off a batsman who goes to make a century that wins the match for the other side. Remember that what you do in the field affects ten team-mates, so you support and back each other up. Fielding can win and lose the game. For instance, the Australian fielding behind the wicket in the 2005 Ashes series was deplorable.

When batting whiz Phil Jaques missed a trip to South Africa for the one-dayers in 2006 that he so richly deserved, chairman of selectors Trevor Hohns said he needed to sharpen up his fielding. Although labelled a 'lame excuse' by Mark Waugh, this emphasises the importance placed upon fielding in the modern game.

Copy the champion fielders, work hard sharpening your skills and concentrate on every ball. The best of the new breed of Australian fieldsmen is Dominic Thornely, of NSW, who can do things that wouldn't be disowned by Jonty Rhodes himself. Of course, I could be accused of bias because I've worked with Dominic since he was a gangling schoolboy in the bush. He says the most valuable lesson he has learned from me is that you spend 85 percent of your time fielding, so why not enjoy it? If it's not fun, you become lethargic.

Wanting to be involved in the game is crucial to playing it well in the field. Reflexes are sharper, the adrenalin pumps harder and the brain works overtime. Thinking negatively dulls your senses.

Dominic, who has the ability to attack the ball by the shortest possible route and throws down the stumps more often than not, can field anywhere from first slip to square leg. At point he's lethal, often bouncing on the balls of his feet instead of walking in with the bowler. I'll let him explain: 'I'm trying to play with the batsman's mind. Some times I'll walk in and some times I won't. If he thinks I'm charging in, he might make up his mind to go hard past me. Or if he reckons I'm standing still, he might drop the ball at his feet and take off for a single. When Stuart MacGill is bowling, I field in a position in front of point that isn't in the textbook. I might appear to be dawdling when he hits his delivery stride, but I'm on the balls of my feet, crouching, ready to go left, right or forward and in position to stop a hard-hit ball or a soft-hit ball. I love fielding at point at the SCG where the wicket gets a bit slower and turns a bit.'

BE FRIENDS WITH THE UMPIRE

Respect the umpires, because if you don't have people willing to stand out in the sun for up to eight hours on a Saturday afternoon, you don't have a game.

It's the most difficult job to do well and please everybody, and in most cases they do an excellent job. Like any batsman, bowler or fieldsman, they make mistakes and there will be times when they raise the finger to give a batsman out when he isn't. It'll balance out, because there will be times when you're given not out when you should be out. As they used to say in the old Wild West saloons, 'Don't shoot the pianist. He's doing his best.'

The dumbest thing a fielding side can do is keep appealing and appealing and try to bulldoze the umpire into giving one of the opposing players out. Why antagonise the guy? He's only human and is hardly likely to do you any future favours.

My players at University of NSW were told to be polite to the umpires, say good morning, respect their decisions and shake hands with them — win, lose or draw — after the match. Most umpires are cricket-nutty people who have never been able to play at this level but love being part of the game and accepted as one of the boys.

Thanks to all the men and women who give up their Saturdays so the players can have a game. I love them. However, keep a wary eye out for the coach of a junior team who doubles up as umpire and will never, ever give a decision against his son. It's a different thing when the gun batsman in the opposing team comes to the wicket. This bloke's finger will shoot skyward at the first opportunity!

People haven't taken many risks with Dominic since he took thirteen catches and brought off nine run-outs in his first season of one-day cricket for the Blues. When it comes to fielding, he has a mind like a steel trap. When he's at point, he'll check the batsman's grip and if it's an open one he knows he really is in the game. If the grip is closed, he'll be lucky to get a catch.

Before the game, Dominic will have briefed his NSW colleagues on the way the various opposing players run between wickets, whether the batsman is slow, how he turns and if he's a nervous runner. Dominic will go to the NSW captain and say, 'Skipper, between us, square leg, mid-on, mid-off and point are going to save you fifteen runs today. Forget about us. Just think about the game and the bowling changes.' Even towards the end of a long day in the field, he's always thinking about what's going to happen with the next ball. No wonder I see him as a future State captain.

In the field, you have to be really alert. I stress the importance of angles, telling how a player can still be in the game when the ball is nowhere near him. It could be a back-up or a relay throw. The great thing about fielding is that you don't have to have the ball in your hand to make a contribution.

Move in as the ball is bowled, take aim before throwing and, when a colleague is throwing, back-up to cover in case the ball is missed at the stumps and there's a danger of overthrows. If you decide that throwing yourself head-first is the best way to stop the ball, it's essential to dive early but beware of going over the top or fumbling.

Be sure to take up the exact position wanted by your captain, marking the spot with your spikes if uncertain. However, if you are not happy about fielding in a certain position, say the slips, it can have a psychological effect that can reduce your performance. Don't hesitate to ask the captain if you can move.

CATCHING

Catches win matches. Drop one and you invite a rival to score a century, while a spectacular catch at exactly the right moment can lift the spirits of a sagging team.

When it comes to catching, the ball should melt into the hands. The size of the hands is not important: it's all about timing. I like the normal method of the hands forming a cup with the fingers pointing upward and little fingers touching. The other method is when the player posi-

Eyes on the ball, balance and soft hands

tions himself right under the ball and the hands are reversed to make a baseball-style catch with the hands still pointing upwards. Jonty Rhodes prefers this method.

The secret of catching in the outfield is to get into a good position to take the ball with nice, soft hands. Do not move until you've judged the flight and length of the ball, and remember that it is easier to run in than run backwards. Keep the head as still as possible and watch the ball all the way into your hands.

Fielding close to the bat calls for razor-sharp reflexes and a lot of practice. Get different angles by throwing the ball off a slip catcher or a roller, or even a tennis ball off a garbage tin. Anticipation is dangerous when you're standing so close to the batsman, so don't go for the ball until it has left the bat. With close-in fielders, I work with a tennis ball before switching to a harder one. The tennis ball is harder to catch. It can be dangerous in close, so we see the guys wearing more gear than Prince Valiant, the knight of old in the Sunday comics. There are helmets, little mini-pads to protect the shin, and who knows what else.

Whenever he could, Dominic Thornely tried to stand next to Mark Waugh in catching practice and attempt to copy his balance and the way the ball never made a sound as it melted into his soft hands. Some people claim Waugh was gifted but somewhat lazy, but Thornely says no. He's emphatic that that nobody caught more balls in training than Mark did. Fielding is all about coordination, which is boosted by lots and lots of hard work. Sir Donald Bradman spent lonely hours as a child hitting a golf ball against a water tank with a stump, while the bricks of the back wall of the Thornely home at Albury are heavily scarred from thousands of cricket and golf balls being smashed into them by a young Dominic.

In the slips, expect every ball to come to you. It's a personal matter whether you keep your eyes fixed on the bowler or the batsman. When I fielded in slips, I used to watch the back of the bat, but do what suits you best. Stand still, head still, knees bent and weight on the balls of your feet.

WAZZA CATCH

From Dominic Thornely down, my pupils have found the Wazza Catch Ball can boost ground fielding and catching skills by sharpening their reflexes and balance. It's simple enough. A tennis ball is attached to a Velcro strap around the wrist by an elastic chord which brings it whizzing back at the thrower from all angles like the old yo-yo. Two things to remember: *always* watch the ball and catch it with two hands.

Dominic Thornely with the Wazza Catch

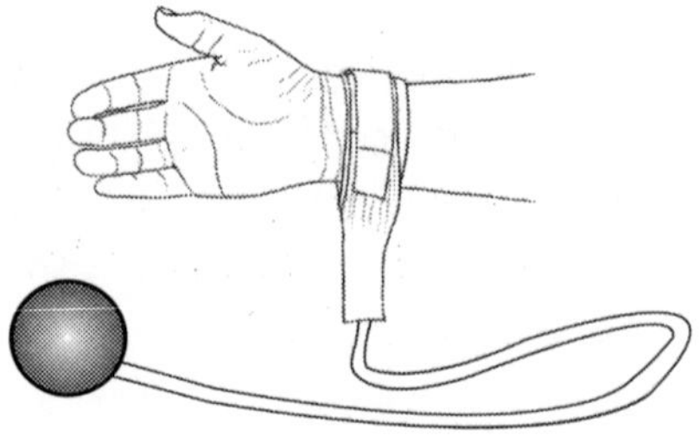

Attach Wazza Catch to wrist using velcro strap. Make sure the elastic cord is on the inside of the palm.

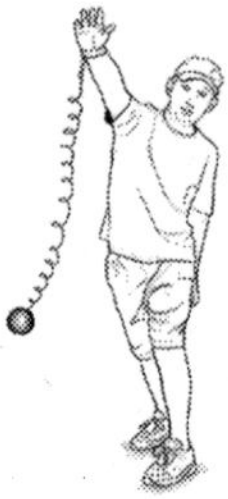

Bowling — Attach Wazza Catch to your bowling arm and proceed to bowl the ball into the ground, catching the return.

Attach Wazza Catch to right wrist and underarm ball away from the body, catching the return with two hands.

Bowling — Try attaching Wazza Catch to your other arm and bowl the ball into the ground, catching the return.

Attach Wazza Catch to left wrist and underarm ball away from the body, catching the return with two hands.

Ground fielding — With the Wazza Catch attached to the right wrist, throw the ball underarm into the ground, making it bounce when retracting. Stay low and take the return in both hands.

Attach Wazza Catch to right wrist and underarm the ball to the right and then left side of the body, catching each return with two hands. Vary the height of the underarm as demonstrated.

Ground fielding — With the Wazza Catch attached to the left wrist, throw the ball underarm into the ground, making it bounce when retracting. Stay low and take the return in both hands.

Attach Wazza Catch to left wrist and underarm the ball to the right and then left side of the body, catching each return with two hands. Vary the height of the underarm as demonstrated.

Throwing — Attach Wazza Catch to your throwing arm and throw the ball into the ground in front and catch the return.

THROWING

As you run in, keep your eye on the ball and the head as still as possible to make sure the ball finishes safely in your hand. Waste as little time as possible in drawing back the arm for a short, sharp throw. Aggressively attack the stumps with the power coming from a cocked wrist and a fast forward swing of the arm. Starting with a stationary ball, hours must be spent practising this below-the-shoulder manoeuvre if you want to perfect it. For the longer throws when accuracy is needed to find the wicketkeeper's gloves, throw over the shoulder with a vertical arm and the elbow high.

PRACTISING

You should train the same way you are going to play. For instance, if there is slip catching practice, it should be done out near the wicket area, so if you drop a ball or miss one, you must chase after it as though it was in a match. Sometimes I take the players to train on a rough ground because it really makes them watch the ball and keep their heads behind it.

BRING IN THE BOUNDARIES FOR THE KIDS

Kids haven't got the strength of grown people, so bring in the boundaries so they can hit fours and sixes. There's nothing better than when your son or daughter comes home and says they scored twenty-five runs. That's much more fun than if they scored five or six runs off six overs largely because the boundaries were too far away. And if the bat is too heavy for them, that makes it even harder.

However, I feel sorry for the bowlers when I see ropes bringing the boundary even closer on English Test and county grounds that are way too small anyway. A hitter like Andrew Flintoff only has to breathe on a ball and it's six.

Eyes glued to the ball

THE SLIDING STOP

Used to cut off balls close to the boundary, the sliding stop allows the fielder more time to get the ball back than the traditional method of stopping the ball with the hand, running past it, turning and throwing it in. Facing the ball as you slide towards it, you can either knock it back or pick it up.

I used to be against the sliding stop, particularly after Ricky Ponting slid into the fence and broke his ankle. However, since they introduced the boundary ropes, the element of danger has been minimised.

WAZZA'S 1% FACTORS

ON FIELD

- Walk onto the field as a team.
- When leaving, the batsmen go first followed by the best players of that session.
- Gather together at the fall of a wicket, sharing the success of the moment.
- Focus on the next ball. It's the only one that counts.
- Get dirty. Throw yourself at the ball if necessary.
- With a positive mindset, move in with the bowler. Want the ball to come to you.
- Attack the ball in the infield, giving the batsman a 'no singles to me' message. Make him feel that he doesn't know from where his next run is coming.
- Relay throws from long boundaries or into the wind, running in pairs to the boundary for the flick back.
- Either bowler, mid-off or mid-on should get to the stumps at the bowler's end, while the wicketkeeper gets to the stumps after every delivery.
- Read the angles to back up throws from other fielders.
- Take care of the ball. It's everybody's responsibility to shine, clean or dry it.
- Try to lift a team-mate who's feeling low. For example, one who's just dropped a catch.
- Make the opposition feel uncomfortable through the positives of the team's bowling and fielding rather than sledging. Make them feel that if they're not at their top, you'll hammer them.
- Move quickly between overs.
- Accept the umpire's decision and get on with the game.

8

CAPTAINCY

'Playing against a team with Ian Chappell as captain turned a cricket match into gang warfare.'

Mike Brearley

According to Richie Benaud, the first requirement for a successful cricket captain is luck. However, by staying two overs ahead of the game you'll find that you make your own luck. And above all, keep it simple.

The thing I like about Australia's Test captains is that they go on the attack from the first ball. If they win the toss, the goal is to score three hundred runs on the opening day to put the opposition on the back foot. They're prepared to risk the possibility of defeat if it means setting up another victory. I liked the way Ian Chappell captained a side because he was such a tough, aggressive bloke who wasn't afraid to improvise and back his judgment. Most importantly, he was honest with his players.

I want my captain to be uncompromising and unselfish, a fierce competitor and natural leader who has presence. He must unquestionably be the boss, and when the players go into the dressing room, everyone waits for him to speak. Can you imagine the aura in which Sir Donald Bradman would have been held by a young player? For the captain

I don't want a guy who yaps and yaps and talks utter rubbish. I want someone like my friend Johnny Lewis, the boxing trainer who mightn't say many words but has presence the like of which I've never experienced.

I don't agree with the school of thought that made Mike Brearley captain of England simply because he was a master tactician. He had to be one as he wasn't much of a bat. The captain should be one of the better players because, the way the game is played today, you can't go into a match virtually one short. With a first-class Masters degree from Cambridge, the bearded Brearley gave out an air of mental superiority rather than aggressiveness in leading the Poms to a series triumph of 5–1 over Australia in 1978/79. In fact, England won the Ashes three times under his captaincy. He typified old-fashioned standards by turning down a big money offer to join the rebel World Series Cricket in the seventies. 'Kerry Packer is not my style,' he said. 'I prefer the chugging British coaster with a cargo of pig-iron to a monstrous supertanker hurriedly constructed.' As you might have gathered, I'm not a Brearley fan, but he did manage to get the best out of Ian Botham.

Ian Chappell was my sort of bloke, a straight shooter who led from the front, not some silky-smooth diplomatic type. He got the last ounce out of Dennis Lillee and Jeff Thomson, had a beer with his team-mates at the end of the day and never ducked the grind of training. The players loved him. He kept an ear open for a suggestion from any of them, particularly wicketkeeper Rod Marsh, and if it made sense, more often than not he'd act on it.

There was the time in Port-of-Spain, Trinidad, in 1973 when Chappell shrugged off a sprained ankle and bad back to score 97 when creasebound on a powdering wicket. At lunch on the last day, the West Indies needed 66 runs with six wickets in hand to take the lead in the series, with the great Rohan Kanhai unbeaten on 91. Throughout the break, Chappell lay motionless on a bench of wooden slats in sauna-like conditions, his face covered by his baggy green Australian cap. He didn't say a word because it is a Chappellism that if you can't say something sensible, then don't say anything at all. When it was time to return to the field, he got up and said bluntly, 'This'd be a bloody good one to win.' Kanhai was out to Max Walker's first ball, the Windies lost 5–21 and Australia went on to win the series 2–0.

Another bloke I'd like to have with me in the trenches is Steve Waugh. He never said much, but like Chappell he was mentally tough and led from the front. They likened him to an iceberg because he was so cool. At the crease Steve lacked the silky smoothness of twin brother Mark, but he played to his limitations and became a very good bat. Some people have accused Steve of being selfish but I won't buy that. Like Doug Walters, he didn't try to farm the strike while batting with a tail-ender, instead sharing it with him. I think that by putting the acid on the batting rabbit like that, it had the effect of giving confidence to him.

Because he got the best out of his players, I thought Mark Taylor was a superb captain. He had beautiful hands, which made him a key man at first slip, and did all the one percent things well. Allan Border was a little nugget who was put into a job he probably didn't want, but he developed into a pugnacious skipper who'd dig Australia out of tight situations. Everybody who was around Richie Benaud raves about his captaincy skills and the way he got 110 percent out of Alan Davidson, one of the most gifted all-rounders of all time. Part gambler, part sorcerer with his leg-spinners and part diplomat, Richie kept it simple as he cajoled men into playing above themselves.

Shane Warne could have made a great Australian captain because he has a fantastic cricket brain. He would have been there for a long time, too, because he doesn't take much out of himself. Sadly, Shane wasn't the off-field role model officials wanted for the second most important job in the country after the Prime Minister, but on the field he's a captain's dream. Simply throw him the ball and let him get on with winkling out the opposing batters.

One of the most ruthless captains I've seen was Clive Lloyd, a gangling chap who loped out to bat for the West Indies with a quizzical look behind his spectacles. After losing a series 5–1 in Australia in 1975/76, he vowed never again to go into a Test without four fast bowlers, and before long the Windies were ruling world cricket with an iron fist. With four murderous quicks taking it in turn to come at the throats of visored, helmeted batsmen, they would bowl their overs at a coldly cynical slow rate, which further added to the pressure. With the ball exploding like a blood-red rocket off the pitch, Lloyd knew how to tighten the screws. With the batsman at the bowler's end hardly anxious to face a rampant Curtly Ambrose or Michael Holding, close-in fielders would be barking away at the batter and Viv Richards prowling like a leopard. 'Settle down, boys,' Lloyd would call from slip in the deepest of voices. Sometimes he'd say as he walked past the batsman, 'How are you going, then?'

WHY ARE MOST CRICKET TEAMS CAPTAINED BY BATSMEN?

There seems to be a mindset in cricket circles that the captain should be a batsman, but I'd like to see more wicketkeepers and bowlers in charge of teams. At least 90 percent of sides these days seem to be captained by batsmen because of a fear that bowlers and stumpers have got enough on their plate as it is. Utter nonsense, of course.

The wicketkeeper is the eyes and ears of a side, but until Adam Gilchrist came onto the scene, Jack Blackham in the 1880s and Barry Jarman in the 1960s were the only keepers who had led Australia. The keeper is in a perfect place from which to captain a side. He has a feel for the game and knows if a batsman is getting edgy or a bowler losing his zing. Rod Marsh, Ian Healy, Darren Berry, Brian Taber, Steve Rixon and Brad Haddin are among the keepers who have led their States in recent years.

Richie Benaud, Ian Johnson and Hugh Trumble were bowlers who have led the men in baggy green caps, while Geoff Lawson did the job magnificently for NSW. Keith Miller should have captained Australia after proving a dashing leader for NSW, but crusty officials feared he might have been too hard to handle. Fast bowlers have been looked upon as a 'bit different', it seems.

WHERE SHOULD THE CAPTAIN FIELD?

The captain must field in a key position, like first or second slip, in the gully or on the drive so he can control the game. No further away because he must be close to the bowler and in the thick of things. Mark Taylor, Bob Simpson and Ian Chappell fielded at first slip where they were marvellous catchers, Richie Benaud and Steve Waugh in the gully. Don Bradman used to be on the drive for much of the time, while Ricky Ponting bobs up in close to grab a blinding catch or engineer a run-out.

From first slip, the captain can see exactly what the bowler is doing, as well as being next to the wicketkeeper. The keeper has a privileged view of what the bowler is doing from how the ball is coming into his gloves and sometimes he can spot a flaw in the batsman's technique that isn't apparent to others. That is part of the keeper's job.

Fielding at first slip, I was an aggressive captain. If I saw a batsman walking to the wicket like Daffy Duck, I'd be straight in the ear of my fast bowler. 'This bloke doesn't want to be here,' I'd say. 'Put him in Disneyland.' If the bowler wasn't having a dip, I'd call from slip, 'Mate, if I want somebody to bowl off-spin, I'll bowl it. I told you this bloke doesn't want to be here. Get rid of him.' Of course, this sort of stuff is par for the course. It's been around since the days of Dr WG Grace.

To get the best out of his team, a captain really must understand the talents and egos of his players and have the ability to communicate. Some guys might be strong-minded individuals, others might be softer types who need a little coaxing, but all of them look to the skipper in a moment of need. They might be bowling and getting hit, or in a slump with the bat. The captain must have tactical inventiveness, a deep knowledge of technical things and an unfailing eye for an opposition's weaknesses. If he can stay a couple of overs ahead of his rivals and enjoy a slice of luck, he'll be a winner.

FIELD PLACING

Always have a reason for your field placing; don't just set a ring field as a matter of course and peg away at the off stump. You build pressure with thoughtful field placing and that is just one of the reasons why Shane Warne has been so good. He bowls to his field. Have a one-in, one-out approach to make the gaps look smaller and put pressure on the batsman. Leave gaps where you want the batsman to hit the ball. For instance, your opening bowler is bowling out-swing, so leave mid-off and mid-on vacant to encourage the drive. With luck, you'll get a nick. However, it's bread and butter for a batsman if the bowler bowls at his pads and he can work the ball away for easy runs.

How much input should a bowler have in setting the field? The bowler is the one with the red rock in his hand, so he should be allowed to set his field first up. However, stress to him that it's his responsibility to bowl to it. Set fields according to the ground on which you're playing. A fast outfield may require a sweeper early in the game, whereas a slow outfield allows the captain to bring fielders closer. If there's a big wicket square, one side of the field can be shorter than the other. On the short side, you'll need a good fielder who's quick across the turf.

BOWLING CHANGES

Be sure to keep your quicks fresh, bowling them in short spells of no more than six or seven overs. Give them a spell before bringing them back for another six, though it all depends upon how the game is going. If the opposing batters are on top, make regular bowling changes to prevent them getting into a rhythm. Switch a bowler to round the wicket, or slow the game down. Make such changes with your head, not your heart, but be willing to back your instincts. If the game is just rolling along, try something new to prevent it becoming stagnant. Be proactive.

One of the problems of South African cricket is that they have long adopted a rigid policy of grinding, robotic tactics. Spin is out while the medium-pacers keep things tight until the spearhead is ready to come back. The field is spread and the bowlers don't over attack. Playing the Proteas, you never expect the unexpected.

THE RUN CHASE

In a run chase, it's crucial not to lose too many early wickets. Don't just go out and blaze away, because you've got to have wickets in hand at the end. There's evidence that a team which loses three or four quick wickets is doomed. Chasing a big score in a one-dayer, don't be frightened to change your normal batting order. You might have an opening bat who simply works the ball around, so if you're set such a target consider bringing up a dasher who usually bats lower in the order as a pinch hitter. An Adam Gilchrist copycat, if you like. Whoever lifted Gilly from No 7 up the order to open the batting in the one-dayers knew what he was about. When the field is up, he simply goes after the ball and hits it over the top.

WHO HAS THE LAST SAY, THE CAPTAIN OR THE COACH?

I set up things up and make a few points, but my captain has the final say when he walks onto the field. He runs the show. We will have discussed how the pitch will play, what to do if he wins the toss, who will be the main attacking and defensive bowlers, and the strengths and weaknesses of the opposition. But it's still up to him.

I had disagreements with David Carson, my captain at University of NSW, because he's got his views and I've got mine. We bounced off each other and usually worked it out. However, there were times when I said 'no' and he went and did it anyway. We respect one another and I saw

IDEAL BATTING ORDER

In a perfect world, the opening pair should be a right-hander and a left-hander who are adept at picking up quick singles, thus forcing the bowlers to change their channel.

Even though the likes of Garry Sobers, Brian Lara, Greg Chappell, Steve Waugh and Allan Border preferred to bat further down the list, I think the best player should bat in the No 3 slot. Whether he goes in at 1–0 or 1–150, the No 3 should have the most input into the shape and character of his team's innings.

Don Bradman batted there, as did Neil Harvey, Viv Richards and Graeme Pollock. The No 3 must be adaptable, able to turn things around or keep the momentum going if the openers have got a bit of a run on.

Greg Chappell was perfect at No 4. With his sound technique and straightest of straight bats, he would have been an ideal choice at No 3 too, but Greg didn't like the position. Besides, brother Ian was filling the spot most capably in Greg's early days in the Australian side. Greg could pick up the runs on offer at No 4 as well as offering the most perpendicular of bats to a ball that was still shiny.

No 5 can get after the bowling a bit, and you want someone who hits them pretty well at No 6. Next comes the wicketkeeper, with Adam Gilchrist unchallenged for this role in any World XI. Still, he has the talent to bat higher than No 7.

Often you'll find a player who starts off in State cricket at No 6 winding up as an opener, with the names of Bob Simpson, Michael Slater, Keith Stackpole and Rick McCosker coming to mind.

him as a miniature Allan Border. He throws like Border, he bats left-handed like Border, he's tough and he doesn't give in. Before the day's play, I used to have a bit of a say before handing over to Carso to have the last word.

Duncan Fletcher, the England coach, is said to operate on the principle that the players cannot have two leaders, so at important moments he defers to the captain Michael Vaughan, allowing him to have the first and last say at team meetings. When Fletcher and a majority of the players won the day in a discussion of whether an injured Nasser Hussain should continue batting with a runner rather than retire, Mike Atherton, the English skipper at the time, commented: 'That could be a costly decision you just made.' The coach said nothing, waiting until that evening to knock on Atherton's door. Fletcher said that, although Atherton may well have been right about Hussain, he should not have spoken to him like that in front of the players. The point was made quietly and unobtrusively.

That was the smart way of doing it, because no coach likes to be downgraded in such a manner. You must pick the moment. Although Carso and I had our differences, the discussion always took place in private. The most important thing a coach can do is not try to captain the side.

WAZZA'S FINAL WORD FOR CAPTAINS

Always be positive. Be in control of your emotions by making your decisions with your head, and don't be frightened to back your instincts. Listen to any advice offered but always make your own decision. Enjoy what you are doing even when things are not going according to plan.

9

PRACTICE, WARM-UPS AND EQUIPMENT

Batting, bowling and fielding are just the tip of the iceberg for a cricketer, as without the proper preparation to sharpen his talents, he'll never reach his potential.

You've got to be prepared, and it starts off the field. I won't tolerate players who waste an opportunity to get worthwhile practice, and I insist on punctuality and everybody wearing the team uniform. The same applies to warm-ups on match day, and if they haven't got the right equipment they may as well forget it.

PRACTICE

Each practice session should have a purpose, whether it is to hone a player's driving or to improve his single-nudging. In the nets, you must simulate match conditions — slogging and fooling about is annoying to bowlers who are trying to work at their technique. With the bat, start slowly as you would in a real game before opening out to play your shots.

WAZZA CRICKET

SET-UP

Four sets of stumps, 20 metres apart in diamond formation. Six pairs of gloves, four batting tees, four bats, four sets of batting gloves, one ball.

PLAYERS

Four batters, four wicketkeepers, two infielders, two outfielders (or four for ten-a-side game).

THE PLAY

- All shots are hit from the batting tee to the off or on side but always between the widest set of stumps.
- The batter is dismissed if the ball is hit outside the stumps or in the air.
- Batters must run anti-clockwise between wickets (hit and run).
- Batters must stay in the crease until the ball is hit.
- Batters must wear batting gloves.
- Batters must set up the ball on a batting tee for each shot (allowing the fielders to reset positions).
- Ball is hit from the tee closest to where it was returned.
- Fielders (infield and outfield) adjust their position to the 'V' direction that the ball will be struck and field the balls by returning to a wicketkeeper.
- Batter scores one point for each successful run taken.

BENEFITS

- Skill development — hitting the ball in the 'V'.
- Advanced footwork (ball–feet).
- Improved fitness.

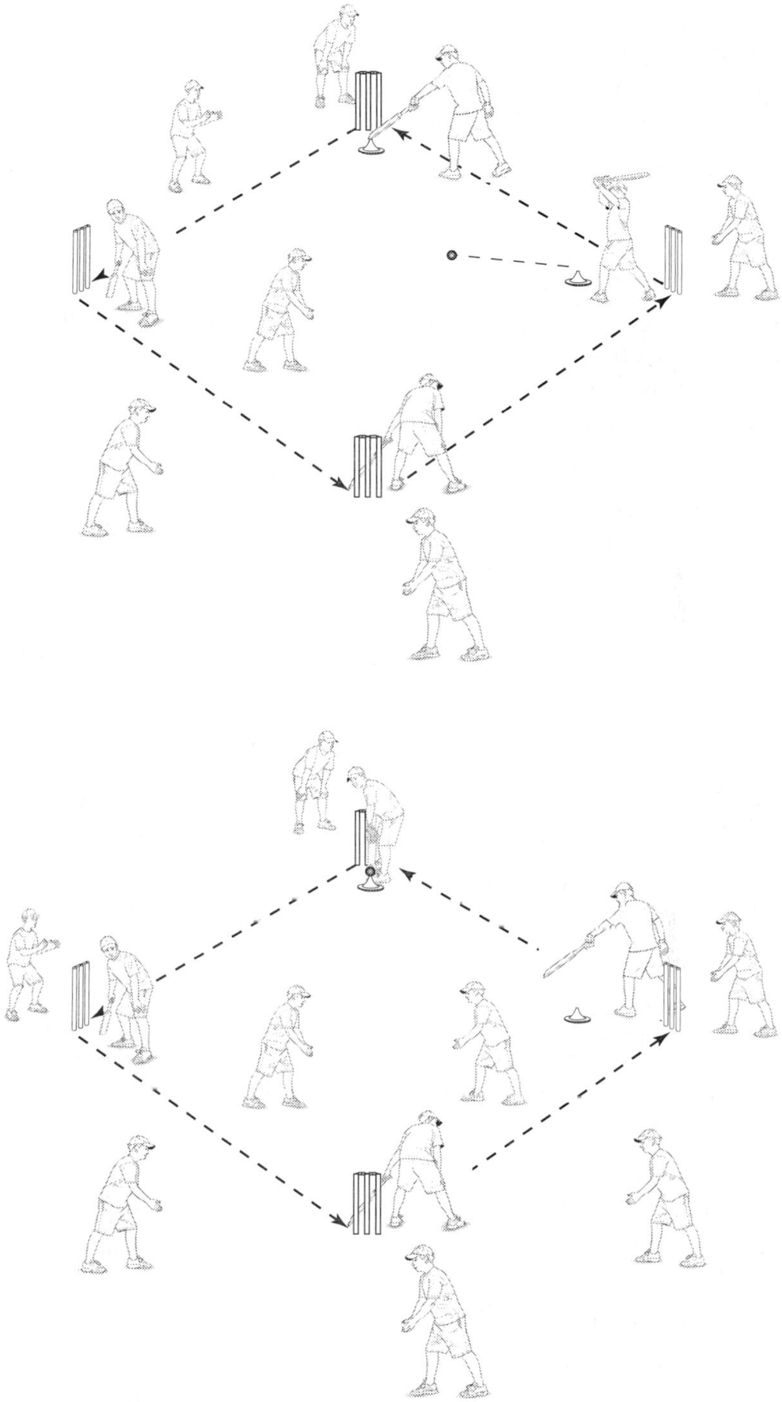

How to play Wazza Cricket

Don't have half a dozen bowlers queuing up to trundle down a succession of balls. Three or four per net is the ideal number as it gives the batsman time between balls to think about the stroke he's just played. The bowlers also have time to concentrate on what they're trying to bowl.

Have a spinners' net rather than mixing them in with the quickish bowlers, and sometimes put in a wicketkeeper behind the spin men so he can get work in a game situation. Let the batters get a rhythm against the quicks, then swap them into the spin net. I want to see bowlers bowling off a fair dinkum run up and it doesn't hurt every so often to have players batting on a wicket that's got a bit of green on it.

Stay alert. If there's a ball on the ground, don't walk past it. Throw it back in with the other kit. Remember what happened to Glenn McGrath in England in 2005 when he trod on a stray ball at practice. He missed two Tests, and that injury could well have cost Australia the Ashes.

Sometimes I put rope ladders on the ground and get the players to hop between the rungs to sharpen their footwork. Another time I might get them playing angles by hitting down the lines of a tennis court or across them, often from off a rubber tee. Wearing batting gloves and with the bat extended in the top hand, they will run up and down juggling balls on the blade in another drill.

Sachin Tendulkar has described a practice net as his laboratory for creating clinical perfection in batting. Before a Test against Australia in Madras, Tendulkar had a practice wicket deliberately roughed up outside leg stump for leg-spinners bowling round the wicket to aim at. When Shane Warne went round the wicket in the match, Tendulkar took him apart, scoring 155 not out.

Sometimes when Dennis Lillee arrived at practice, he'd look for the oldest ball he could find rather than bowl with a scarcely-used Kookaburra which would bounce more because it was harder. He wanted a ball that he could make work.

WARM-UPS

At the University of NSW, we had practice sessions on Tuesdays and Thursdays and got together for thirty or forty minutes each Friday at 6 pm sharp at Coogee Beach. We had a swim, played a game of touch footy, threw each other in the water, played some beach cricket and perhaps even sneaked a peek at a pretty girl in a bikini. Then we went for a meal and discussed the events of the next day. It helped keep us together and got the boys really focused on the coming game. I might have said to our opening bowler, Tim Lang, 'You're the man, Langy. There might be a bit of juice in the wicket tomorrow. I want you in their face.' It gave him something to think about overnight.

On match day I like my players to get to the ground an hour and a half before the start and I'll be there an hour earlier to get all the stuff ready for them. 'Good morning boys,' I'll say. 'Ready to go?'

I like the warm-ups to be short and sharp, really quality stuff maybe lasting half an hour. This is followed by another twenty minutes after the captains have tossed.

The warm-ups start with some jogging, perhaps tossing a footy about, and a really good stretch against the fence and exercises on the ground. The emphasis is on getting the hamstrings and lower back nice and loose before a light-hearted game of touch. The players take it in turns to run the drills, with the guy in charge told the day before that he'll be doing it. After that they might have a quick game with a tennis ball or even a footy for eight minutes to further liven them up. The players then start a program of fielding, with high catches and short fielding.

I hit tennis balls (coloured, but never yellow ones) because they float, and if you can catch one you can catch any ball that's ever been invented. Even in the dressing room, the guys warm up by throwing tennis balls against the wall. Batsmen do this with their pads and gloves on to help get their focus and their feet moving.

If it's a two-day game, the drills vary. It's a different warm-up from that done on the first morning to that on the second day depending on whether we're batting or bowling.

If the captain comes back after the toss and says, 'We're batting,' the first four batters have a hit against some throw-downs, but if we're bowling the guys break up. The wicketkeeper will take the quicks and, when I was at the University of NSW, my assistant Rod 'Scorch' Evans would work with the spinners. Then we're ready to go. I love to work with good people. Scorch and team manager Peter Richardson, who loves his cricket almost as much as a vintage red, were irreplaceable.

When we do the fielding drills, I want the guys switched on and ready to go. I hate sloppiness and will not have slip catching where the catchers are backed by a fence that stops a missed ball. We go out in the centre, and if a guy puts one down he has to run and fetch it. However, when you hit high catches, stand in the middle and hit towards the fence.

I do everything in a game situation. With the slip catching, I'll do the left-handed nicks as I'm left-handed and Scorch would do the right-handed ones, so the guys are getting catches at different angles as you would when a right-hander is batting with a left-hander. We do bat-padders, too, everything to give them an awareness of what might happen.

I watch the other team doing their warm-up on the other side of the ground, and if they're getting about like Brown's cows I tell my blokes, 'Look at them, boys. We've come to play. They haven't.'

WAZZA TIP

WHY I HAVE A BICYCLE IN THE DRESSING ROOM

I got the idea watching an American gridiron match on TV when I saw one of the players riding a bike on the sideline in a bid to shrug off an injury. It started me thinking.

How many times do you see a batsman sit there for three hours watching two of his colleagues figure in a long partnership, then a wicket falls and he's out almost as soon as he gets to the wicket? Sitting on his backside for so long, he becomes dozy rather than mentally alert.

So I get the waiting batsman, still wearing his pads, to hop on the bike and pedal away for a couple of overs. His legs are going and the mind and body snap back into action. Otherwise he might walk out to the non-striker's end, take off and be run out without facing a ball.

It's the same with a bowler, especially a quick. If he's been out in the field and comes off for the tea break with the captain planning to bowl him from the top end when they go back, the first thing is for him to have a bit of fluid. Then he jumps onto the bike to get his legs into gear.

Dominic Thornely rides the bike

I want the players, especially the bowlers, to drink plenty of fluids before they go out for the warm-ups, particularly if it's a hot day. After the quicks have done their warm-ups, and are cooling down, they *must* continue to do stretches. I once spoke to Dennis Lillee about this. When he was at his peak, he'd bowl in the nets for an hour before play and head back to the dressing room with sweat pouring off him. He'd shower, put on a clean shirt and he was ready to go. With the wear and tear that came later in his career, he cut back and didn't do as much. When it all boils down, cricket is a pretty commonsense game in which players must take responsibility for looking after their part of the operation.

I won't tolerate an opening bowler who says, 'I don't come good until my third over.' That's rubbish. I say to the bloke if he's not going to be fair dinkum straight away, warmed up and wanting to take a wicket with his first ball, he might as well not go out there. That's like a guy getting into a car and saying he'll be right at the third traffic light. By then he could have been wiped out. It's the same with an opening bat who takes the field with the preconceived idea of blocking the first ball. If he can work it and pick up a single, isn't that better?

I like players who are not batting to watch the game, checking which of the other team has a weak arm or what to expect from the various bowlers. If it's really hot, I don't like guys to sit out in the sun, but if they do they should be wearing a hat, preferably one with a wide brim and not that silly back-to-front cap that Lleyton Hewitt wears. And I want the fast bowlers to be given a drink on the boundary if they're in the middle of a spell and losing fluid.

Preparation starts in the dressing room. The guys know that everything they need is there. The bicycle in case the next batsman in wants to hop on to retain his focus while he waits his turn during a long partnership. A skipping rope, too, but the player keeps his pads on while he rides or skips. There are tennis balls to throw against the wall and catch, and even a racket to hit them.

Here's how it works. Wearing pads and gloves, throw a ball against the wall and move from side to side while catching it. Get the body and hips moving, so if you get a short one early you'll be more inclined to get inside and hook it. A good stretch at this stage is to put the bat behind the top of your shoulders and get the hips moving as you sway from side to side. When you go out to bat, look up into the sun to get your eyes focused and check the field. I call them the one percent factors and there are lots of them. Not only do I want the better batters to ride the bike and skip, but also the blokes who bat nine, ten and eleven. They might not be as gifted as the first five or six, but I get them on the bike because one of them might hit up the extra twenty runs that get us over the line.

WAZZA'S 1% FACTORS

OFF FIELD ON MATCH DAYS

- Be punctual.
- Warm up as a team, with plenty of talk and encouragement. Let the opponents know your team is here to compete.
- Sit together, enjoying each other's company and supporting the two batsmen at the crease.
- Vocally support a great shot or an individual milestone, such as fifty or a century.
- Congratulate each other's successes.
- Positive talk only. No talking up the opposition or talking down our team.
- Dress appropriately in the team uniform whether at practice or a match.
- Sun protection at all times.
- Hydrate well before the start of play and get a drink during breaks.
- Trust and respect your team-mates.
- The twelfth man always dresses in white.
- The thirteenth man is to get drinks around the boundary for bowlers.
- Clean playing clothes and training gear at all times.
- Warm down as a team.

EQUIPMENT

Doting parents buy too much of the wrong gear for young boys and girls, with bats that are too heavy and pads that are too big. It's crazy to buy a bat for a kid with the thought that it's going to last for six years, so he'll grow into it. It will be too big and heavy and the child will struggle to swing it as it will feel like a tree with the branches lopped off. He needs a light bat because his body hasn't developed. It's the same with pads, which mustn't be too big to impede swift footwork.

I do think each child from eight to ten should have a helmet as a safety measure. It's the same in rugby, where you see kids aged five and six wearing headguards, even the wingers. When they get a helmet, they should wear it around the house to get used to moving about with it on. It's the same with brand-new pads and batting gloves. If the pads aren't moulded to your legs, rashes and sores can result, so wear them at home for a while before strapping them on for a game.

How things have changed! When I was a kid, you used the team pads and your own bat was a thing to be treasured. Who can forget the wonderful smell of linseed oil when you applied it to the bat at the start of the season? Now there's so much stuff out there, most of it coming from India. Such a variety of bats that one suspects that many of them come out of the same factory with a different sticker applied.

Cricket bats are big business. For example, Michael Clarke supposedly signed a million-dollar contract to use a Slazenger bat. Puma, Gray-Nicolls, Gunn & Moore and Kookaburra are among the other leading brands. Most of the leading players carry three or four bats in their coffin bag, with Justin Langer having as many as five. Mike Hussey has two for practice and two for matches.

Bigger bats with deep, thick edges and a slight bow at the bottom are in, with Adam Gilchrist using one weighing 2 lb 9 oz or 2 lb 10 oz. He says he isn't super-fussy, like Justin Langer, Ricky Ponting or Matthew Hayden, about his bats, content largely to use whatever the manufacturer comes up with.

Ponting dotes on the thick-edged model and cuts the knob off the top of the handle of his bat to make it a little shorter. His Kookaburra bat weighs 2 lb 10 ½ oz. Big hitter Andrew Symonds' bat has a longer-than-usual blade with thick edges that weighs 2 lb 10 oz.

Like Michael Clarke, Langer uses a thin-handled bat, one with plenty of grains and hopefully a 'butterfly' imperfection in the wood, which he thinks is lucky. Langer says parents should not be put off buying such a

Wazza checks out Dominic Thornely's gear

bat for their child because the butterfly knot isn't an indication of weakness in the wood. When Justin first came into the Australian side he was ribbed about his 2 lb 5 oz bat, but now he wields a 2 lb 9 oz one with the fashionable thick edges.

Lisa Sthalekar, a slip of a lass who is an important player for Australia and captains the NSW Breakers, admits she once fell into the trap of buying a heavy bat she could hardly lift. Like so many young girls starting out, she thought she needed such a bat if she was going to hit boundaries. Now Lisa uses a 2 lb 5 oz Gray-Nicolls model which is perfect for her style of accumulating runs rather than blasting them.

A cricketer spends so much time in his or her boots that they must be nice and comfortable. If you're serious about the game, you should have a couple of pairs, with fast bowlers needing three.

The ambitious wicketkeeper needs two pairs of good comfortable gloves, plus inner gloves. According to Alan Campbell, a former State squad keeper who is manager of the NSW High Performance unit, buying gloves is like getting a new pair of shoes. They must fit perfectly, with the hands fitting snugly right down into each finger of the glove so if you throw the ball back or dive for a ball, the glove is not going to fall off. Check that the padding on your new gloves covers the fleshy part at the base of your fingers, down the side of the hand under the little finger and underneath the thumb.

TIP

When you get a new pair of gloves, tape a ball into each catching cup overnight, thus helping to form a mould of your hands around the ball.

Once the inners had to be soaked in water, but not any more. The light mini-pads are excellent because they allow much more freedom of movement. Wanting to be even quicker, Ray Phillips once kept in a one-dayer in Brisbane wearing no pads at all.

Cricket gear has become a mind-boggling business. In the big stuff, openers go out wearing a helmet, pads, an arm-protector, box, thigh pad and, if the bowler is really quick, chest guard. Add the bat and it's a wonder they can sprint through for a quick single. The fielder standing at bat-pad is wearing a helmet and probably a box and mini-pads.

Just remember: there's no point in having the most expensive top-of-the-range gear if it doesn't fit to your body.

DON'T USE YOUR FAVOURITE BAT AGANST A BOWLING MACHINE

With the bowling machine firing down balls that often are rock-hard one after another, take an old bat into the net with you. I've seen dozens of broken handles and broken edges, particularly if the user is a hard hitter. With bats today being made from a lighter, softer wood, those hard yellow balls made from nylon are bat-breakers.

10

FITNESS

As our cricketers undertake a schedule that would make the Labours of Hercules seem a childish chore, fitness gurus like slim, trim Andrew May are helping to keep our players one step ahead of their rivals.

Swiss balls have become a familiar sight in the gym, yoga and pilates are part of the training regimen, and May and his colleagues work on a core strength program aimed at strengthening the stomach and lower back and so reducing the risk of injury to the groin, hamstrings and lower back.

Few cricket fans would have heard of Andrew May, a strength and conditioning coach who works with the Australian and NSW players, but his efforts behind the scenes are crucial. Each player has an individual program depending upon the role he fills. With the intensity of the game having lifted so sharply, a strong base of fitness and health is crucial so players don't tumble off the treadmill of playing and travel.

Andrew was a middle distance runner who moved from Tasmania to set up shop in Sydney after just failing to achieve his dream of representing

Australia in the 1500 metres at the 2000 Olympics. He'd been a personal trainer working in corporate health, so the logical step was to start such a business in Sydney. Andrew started working with Cricket NSW four years ago and went to England with Ricky Ponting's Australians in the second half of the Ashes tour in 2004. He is also sought after to speak and work in corporate health.

The players swear by the methods of this articulate chap, who was happy to share his secrets of fitness and diet with me, particularly when applied to the players below the elite level who want to improve their fitness and consequently their game.

'It used to be just weights,' says Andrew, 'but the intensity of the game has lifted so much that now it's about getting the whole athlete conditioned and ready. You give them a balance of upper body work, abdominal work, lower body work and a lot of arm balance work, too. We work on wobble boards, with guys closing their eyes so the balance factor switches on. You can have someone who's super-strong but they might not be able to stand on their own two feet properly when they run in and bowl a ball. The wobble board provides the link between balance, stability and strength.'

Before moving to the top end where the elite players are highly paid professionals who devote a lot of their time to training, let's look at how the average club player can get fitter. If he can do this, he'll play more games and have a better chance of getting to a higher level where he'll receive top coaching. From there he's more likely to be picked for representative teams and then State and national sides.

It's hard for the club player because he hasn't got the time and often the facilities and is more prone to injury. Andrew May suggests the following fitness program for the ambitious club cricketer.

SWIMMING

'I'd like them to have a pool session early in the week, anything from 500 metres to a kilometre depending on how good a swimmer they are. If they play on Saturday and don't have a game the next day, swim on Sunday. If they play both days, swim on the Monday. The pool work should be accompanied by a really good stretch.'

STRENGTH WORK

'Go to the gym and do one strength session a week, ideally involving eight to ten different exercises. Chin-ups, squats and bench presses on a

Swiss ball as well as single leg squats, abdominal work, shoulder exercises and a lot of rotator cuff and stability work.'

RUNNING OR BIKE RIDING

'On another day it would be good to do a run or a bike ride, with some sprints in there as well. However, it's not a matter of distance. Put a time on it, say about thirty to forty minutes. It's more of a speed session than a plod.'

HOW MUCH?

'As an absolute minimum, I'd like the club player to do one swim, at least one weight session and one fitness or speed session. If they do this on top of their club training, they'll be delighted with their improved level of fitness. When players come into the Under 17, Under 19 and Colts programs, we tend to more generic programs purely because you don't get to spend as much time with them. As they progress even higher and mature a bit more, they are given an individual program.'

Now let's hear what Andrew May has to say about the working life of the elite player as they seek to get fitter, sharper and stronger away from the crowds and the big arena. They need to be able to play at the top level, especially in Twenty20 games that are so quick and dynamic over three hours.

FAST AND MEDIUM-FAST BOWLERS

'Cricket is a unilateral sport with a predominance on one side, so a right-hand bowler is going to come in, plant the right foot and bowl with all his weight on the left foot coming in. So he has to be really, really strong on that back right hip and have shoulder strength and stability all over, but especially on the right side. Good balance through the ankles, too.

'We must make sure such bowlers are super-strong from the hips, through the core, the abdominal region and lower back, calling for lots and lots of stability work rather than heaps of heavy lifting in the gym. We do a lot of technique work between strength, balance and stability. With fast bowlers, firstly we must make sure they have a good running technique because if they come into the crease with the hips low and shoulders everywhere, they're not going to optimise their skills.

'We try to get them fit enough to go into a Test match in really hot weather and bowl twenty overs in a day as well as running about in the field.'

BATSMEN

'Running technique is not as important because they're scampering between wickets. We obviously look at speed, but we want reaction time so they can take off quickly from the mark. We call that first-step quickness. Agility is important, too, as it's no good if they're quick but can't turn quickly and go back to the other end.

'Batsmen also need to do a lot of work on strength and stability, particularly on the Swiss ball, which provides an unstable base. In the gym, mainly in the off season, they do single leg squats, medicine ball work, chin-ups and upper body work. In the season, we try to get them to do weights every seven to ten days, but this is dictated by their playing schedule. Not heavy weights, though, because we don't want absolute strength. The heaviest of the players would squat around 100 kilograms. Cricket is a game that might go for a day or five days, so we're after muscle endurance and power. The guys are doing more stability and endurance-type work.

'Batsmen, especially the higher-order ones, need to have a strong aerobic base or cardiovascular fitness because they might be out in the middle for four or five hours. That's when they draw on that fitness base and link it with concentration. How do they build such a base? Although some guys start doing their own thing in May, we start as a squad in June doing more longer running, bike riding, swimming and maybe a bit of running. Yoga, too. About eight weeks out from when the season starts in October, we start specialising, with batters, bowlers and keepers doing specific work.'

STRETCHING

'One of cricket's traditions is that players warm up before the start of play and then go back to the room. However, when the fast bowlers return, we make sure they keep moving and stretching to keep warm as long as they possibly can. We don't want them sitting down and losing all the benefits of the warm-up. Brett Lee will jump about, fire himself up with music and maybe have a leg massage before he goes out. Because everyone is different, other players might sit quietly and reflect on what lies ahead. Justin Langer and Matthew Hayden indulge in yoga or meditation to relax before they go out to bat.'

WARM DOWN

'At the start of the day, the stretching should be dynamic and fast to simulate the movement the players will need when they take the field. At the end of play, it is aimed at recovery. At the elite level, the Aussie guys play so much that a really good stretch and a light pool session is very important.'

DIET

'There's food we should eat more and food we should eat less. A couple of serves of good, lean protein a day is a must. For breakfast, you might have eggs or some yoghurt, for lunch a sandwich with chicken or tuna and for dinner a portion of lean meat. However, a couple of helpings of red meat a week is sufficient. Choosing as many different colours as possible, you should be having at least five different vegetables a day and two servings of fruit. Rather than all yellow veggies, have some capsicum, peas and carrots.

'Avoid deep-fried food, chocolate, cakes, pastries and saturated fats. If players who are hovering at the elite level are overweight, it's going to hold them back. They are going to tire quicker and are more likely to suffer injuries. To sum up, eat good food in moderation. It's part of the culture of cricket to have a beer with your mates, but we talk to the guys about drinking in moderation, eating the right things and getting plenty of sleep to get that balance outside the game.'

FLUIDS

'When Gatorade did some sweat tests with the Australian players, Adam Gilchrist was found to lose more than a litre and a half per hour. That's a lot. If Adam is out there batting for two or three hours and he's not replacing it, he'll definitely become dehydrated. When it's hot and muggy, if you sweat a lot, you need half a litre or a litre every hour to keep your fluids up.'

WHO ARE THE FITTEST?

'There are different types of fitness, but for power and natural strength Andrew Symonds stands alone. Brett Lee is super-fit with all the real stuff needed for a fast bowler, and Michael Hussey is also very fit. Adam Gilchrist is superbly fit as far as the specifics for a wicketkeeper are concerned. Look at Shane Watson with his shirt off and he looks like a Greek statue. He's one of those mesomorph types who only have to pick up a weight to put on muscle.'

PROMPT TREATMENT OF INJURY

If an injury is treated promptly, it can cut weeks from the time a player is on the sidelines. Team managers should have a first aid kit on hand and a source of ice nearby to begin treatment immediately. Don't wait until the end of the day. The players most at risk are quick bowlers, who can break down with lower back or hamstring problems.

You don't fool around with injuries, so you couldn't do better than seek the advice of Greg Craig, who performed a string of minor miracles as physiotherapist for the Wallabies for almost twenty years. One of Australia's most prolific scoring batsmen surely would have been forced to quit cricket but for Craig's work on his dodgy knees at his Narrabeen clinic, while two of the world's most famous tennis players are other grateful clients.

Craig has three golden rules when a sportsman suffers an injury: apply ice as quickly as possible, don't apply heat and don't drink alcohol the night you suffer an injury. Greg says bluntly, 'Drinking is out after you've suffered a muscle injury because alcohol causes vaso-dilation of the blood vessels.' Here's how Greg treats some of the more common injuries:

Lower back: Ice it and get an anti-inflammatory to settle the injury down. Then see a sports physician or sports physio as soon as possible. Invariably the fast bowler suffers back problems and none is immune. Dennis Lillee's career was nearly wrecked by back injuries and Brett Lee is another who has had back problems. Geoff Lawson, too.

Hamstring: Ice for twenty minutes and start gentle stretching as soon as possible. Then some light exercising, but the moment there is pain, stop.

Corked thigh: Elevate the leg and, bending the knee as far as possible, ice the cork for twenty minutes every two to three hours. Start contracting the quadracep muscle until pain returns.

Ankle sprain: Keep icing for twenty minutes every two to three hours to reduce the swelling. Absolutely no heat. Start some balance exercises as soon as possible. Strapping can help, too.

THE MOST IMPORTANT THING TO REMEMBER

Andrew May: 'Don't neglect your strengths. Too many players focus solely on their weaknesses at the expense of making their strengths even stronger. Perhaps you have great endurance but are not quick off the mark. Don't spend all your time searching for that extra zip, because it may not happen. Likewise, some players are really quick and dynamic but can't run a five-kilometre time trial. No matter. Stick with your strengths.'

11

LEARN FROM THE CHAMPIONS

Every cricket champion is different, and we can learn something from all of them. To finish up, I'd like to share my thoughts on some of the game's greatest.

PLAYERS WITH CLASS

I like Ricky Ponting's aggressiveness. He's a terrific player square of both sides of the wicket when the ball is short. Like Ian Chappell, he's quick to take up the challenge, and if the ball is there to hook he'll hook it, a philosophy I like. If there's no-one around, then give it a go. However, if a bowler starts popping down the short ones with a couple of guys on the fence, it can be a simple get-out shot. You've got to be smart about it. Remember Andrew Hilditch, who opened the innings for Australia a few years back? They called him the Happy Hooker because the West Indians would ping the ball in short and there would be a guy at fine leg waiting to swallow the catch. Ponting has been a wonderful player, but bowlers who move the ball around a bit can square him up.

Every team needs a patient, focused player like Justin Langer at the top of the order. He'll nudge the ball around until he gets into the 'zone' that players talk about and then puts on a spurt by going for the big, aggressive shots. Langer's concentration is backed by a lot of character and courage. A few years ago he was washed up, but ground his way back in 2001 with a century against England at The Oval. His determination to improve borders on the fanatical, and mentally he's as solid as Uluru.

Adam Gilchrist is a special talent but he's so unorthodox that I wouldn't advise any kid to try to do it his way. When I did a clinic at Wollongong, I saw a lot of the boys batting with their hands held high on the handle like Gilly. Their feet were tucked in a bit and they leaned the way he does. The kids had been watching Adam and, because he was their hero, they copied his whip-wristed style. I love the way Gilchrist backs himself. Australia can be 5–63 when he walks to the wicket and you almost can see him saying to himself, 'I'm going for it.' Gilly just tees off with his chunky 2 lb 10 oz bat, and if he's there for thirty overs you know what's going to happen. In a way Gilchrist reminds me of Keith Miller, the devastating player who'd open the bowling for Australia, grab a blinding catch at first slip or score a hundred batting up the order. Gilly is an all-rounder, too, a wicketkeeper who opens the batting in the one-dayers and bats at seven in the Test matches. He's good enough to play solely as a bat, and if he continues to struggle with his knees you could bat him at five or six and bring in Brad Haddin to do the keeping. I'm surprised they don't lift Gilly up the order if Australia is 3–270 and the other team's backside is on the ground. Using a pinch-hitter never seems to work, but a stroke-player like Gilchrist will always do more damage than a bloke who just goes out and slogs.

By bowling well within himself, Glenn McGrath is so accurate, staying in that corridor just outside off stump and waiting for the batter to make the fatal mistake. With his control and a high action, which can generate awkward bounce, he's a machine. There will be subtle variations of pace, bounce and angle as he unlocks the batsman's technique and adds another wicket to his portfolio. Left-handed batters hate him. 'Pigeon' looks after himself, going through his stretches and making sure he does all the right things to avoid injury. He probably has been helped by being a late starter who wasn't bounding in at the age of twelve trying to bowl fast, particularly considering those rock-hard run-ups at his home town of Narromine, a small farming town north-west of Sydney.

The control of Ricky Ponting

Shane Warne is like a cat playing with a mouse when he takes the ball. A player hits a four and you can almost hear him chortling, 'Ha, ha, ha. How are you going mate? Going all right are you? Gee, what's on tonight? Won't be here long, will you?' Like Muhammad Ali in boxing, Shane is the greatest. Every year he announces to the cricketing world that he's developed a new mystery ball but it's all bluff. I could sit and watch Warne for hours. He doesn't bounce up to the crease, simply waddles in and drops straight into a length. Shane is all shoulder and rips the ball in with very strong wrists, and because he doesn't take much out of himself with his action he could bowl for another ten years if he wants to. Young players should try to emulate his phenomenal control and uncomplicated method.

Sachin Tendulkar's nimble footwork is the key to his success. With eyes glued to the ball, the Indian champion gets into position so quickly to play a shot. Small and sturdy, he's as technically perfect as a player can be, and generates extraordinary bat speed. As a child, he spent hours hitting a ball suspended in a sock. Until I went to India in 2005, I didn't realise how the expectations of a billion Indians depend upon how Tendulkar performs. When he bats, you see his compatriots crammed round fuzzy television sets and crackly radios hoping and praying their hero will conquer the world. Sir Vivian Richards claims he used to deliberately smash the ball straight back at the bowler to frighten them, and Tendulkar is the same. In fact, when the great Dennis Lillee was asked in India how he would bowl to Tendulkar, he quipped, 'With a helmet on.' A video, made for Sir Donald Bradman's ninetieth birthday party, to which Tendulkar was invited, showed the two men playing the same shot simultaneously on a split screen. The similarities of body position and bat angles were said to have been uncanny. During a rare television interview, the Don said, 'Watching Tendulkar on TV, I was very struck by his compactness, his stroke production and his technique — it all

The determination of Justin Langer

seemed to gel. I never saw myself play, but I feel that this fellow is playing much the same way I used to.'

The West Indian Brian Lara has an extravagantly high backlift, a little too big for my liking. I worry about his big backlift when things aren't running smoothly, because it leaves him open to being yorked or nicking a Glenn McGrath delivery to gully. Yet, like Tendulkar, Lara gets into position in an instant. When he's in the zone, the ball goes magnificently off his bat and he can be nigh unstoppable, as his world-record Test score of 400 not out would indicate.

THE DON

What can we learn from Sir Donald Bradman, the greatest run-maker there has ever been? Well, the main thing is that you never attempt to change a genius. Simply build on what he's got. Bradman's figures speak for themselves: a Test average of 99.94 (the next best figure is 60.97), a first-class average of 95.14, and a century every third time he went out to bat.

From a technical point of view, Sir Donald did everything wrong by the coaching book. You can't coach the way he played, but he had two sharp eyes and unbelievable footwork. Bradman was light as a feather on his feet, skipping to the pitch of the ball like a ballroom dancer.

We always say that the batsman should put his foot to the ball but, although Bradman's foot was away from it, his head was over the ball when he hit it. Garry Sobers was another unorthodox freak. With players like Bradman and Sobers, who were very special, you simply let them go and try to build on their strengths.

Because Bradman stood with the bat inside his back foot instead of behind it, the bat would come into the ball from more angle than was advisable, but when he hit it, it would be with the full face of the blade. According to the purists, when you do your pick-up the bat should go straight towards off stump or first slip. Largely because he batted with the bat between his feet, Bradman's blade went in the direction of second slip but he was a law unto himself. Don't go wider to gully, because your hands start moving wrongly.

The art of coaching is to build on what the guy has got. Take Andrew Flintoff's extremely wide stance. It's not a problem for him, because when he hits the ball he shows it the full face of the bat. And when he hits it, it stays hit. When Flintoff played Shane Warne you could almost hear him say, 'I'll block this one,' as he bent his front knee and back leg and sent the ball away for a single from a simple defensive shot. England's small grounds aren't big enough to contain a hitter like Flintoff, because if the ball was dropped a bit short at the vast Melbourne Cricket Ground he'd hit it into Bay 15.

People suggest that Bradman would not have been able to set his records today, but that's rubbish. They wouldn't have been able to hold him, particularly in the one-day stuff. He batted on uncovered wickets and didn't have a helmet and other protective clothing when he faced the thunderbolts of Englishman Harold Larwood in the Bodyline series of 1932. His hand-eye coordination was unbelievable, the result of long hours of back-yard practice spent hitting a golf ball against a water tank with a cricket stump.

IN CLOSING

One last word for the budding coach: whatever you do, don't turn a player into a robot by curbing his natural talents. At the start with Michael Slater, I worked on getting his defence and stance right so nature could take its course as he got older. Then I concentrated on strengthening his strengths.

Would Doug Walters have ever got a run if somebody had told him the cut shot was too risky? Likewise if the coach had told Ian Chappell or Ricky Ponting to give the hook shot away. Learn from the champions by all means, but don't be a total copycat.

WAZZA TIP

I do use bowling machines but I'm not big on them, because they're too repetitive, producing the same ball every time rather than letting a batsman face balls coming from different angles.

When Bradman came to Sydney from the bush, the State coach at the time threw up his hands when he saw his grip and the way he shaped up with the bat between his feet. This meant that when he was at the crease he took the bat back towards second slip. 'You'll never get a run in first-class cricket unless you change it,' said the coach. Bradman didn't change it, and he did get a run or two.

It was the same with Bill O'Reilly. When the famed leg spinner Arthur Mailey saw him at a State practice session, he told Bill he must change his grip of the ball if he wanted to succeed at the top level. Bill ignored the advice and became a champion.

There's a lesson to be learned here. Although I'm not suggesting youngsters should ignore the advice of their coach, I believe they must never be frightened to back their talent.

ACKNOWLEDGMENTS

The list is endless. Firstly, thanks to my wife Pam, who puts up with it all. I've rarely been happier than in the old days when we put the bowling machine and other cricketing gear into the back of my battered blue ute and combined a coaching trip through the bush with a family holiday with our kids, Bradley and Brylee.

I'm so grateful to the wonderful game of cricket. If Michael Slater hadn't turned up at one of my coaching clinics at the age of seven, this book would never have eventuated and I could not have shared his exhilarating climb to the top of the cricketing world. I've been there through the tough times, too, and I'm proud of the way Michael has carved out a new career for himself as a commentator. My other prize pupil Dominic Thornely is such a deep thinker about the game that I see him as a future NSW captain and hopefully he'll get a baggy green cap as well.

Apart from this pair, I'd like to thank my co-author, Terry Smith. (It's a funny thing but Terry and I share the same birthday: 10 November.) Also Geoff Lawson, for whom I have enormous respect as he never sugarcoats his opinions, Dominic Thornely, Phil Jaques, Brad Haddin, Alan Campbell and David Freedman, all of whom helped Terry and I in putting my thoughts down on paper.

Photographer Mark Evans added a further dimension with his professionalism with the lens. While working on this book, Mark followed up his 1999 Walkley Award by winning a World Press Photo Award in Amsterdam with his wife Jenny. Greg Craig, who worked miracles with the Wallabies for almost twenty years, happily gave us the clues for prompt treatment of injuries, and fitness guru Andrew May provided an intriguing insight into how our elite players achieve a peak level of fitness. I owe them all a large drink.

Thanks to Neil McDonald, Peter Spence, Graham Gorrel of the *Daily Advertiser* in Wagga, Ross Turner and Ross Elliott, who encouraged me to push ahead with my coaching career, and all the players and coaches with whom I've traded observations, often deep into the night. Some are household names, others are not.

I am indebted to Sachin Bajaj, the engaging Mr Fixit who runs the World Cricket Academy in India. When I suffered my third heart attack in Mumbai in 2005, in almost an instant he had me whisked to the bed which had been occupied by the Prime Minister in the city's main hospital and attended by the PM's surgeon, Dr Gawel, a tall, distinguished man who wore a bow tie.

And not forgetting bright, innovative Ali Lavau for editing with such expertise and support, and copy editor Michael Wall, who has been particularly helpful and helpfully particular.

Warren Smith,
WAGGA WAGGA, 2006

TERRY SMITH

Terry has spent a lifetime as a sports scribbler, starting as a teenager when he was ghost writer for world champion boxer Jimmy Carruthers at the old Sydney Stadium. In 2000 he was awarded the Australian Sports Medal for services to sports writing, with his sixteen previous books including *The Bedside Book of Cricket Centuries*.

Terry has covered a host of world boxing titles, rugby union Tests and major golf championships in all parts of the world for newspapers in Sydney. His last book was *The Champions and The Courses They Played*, a history of the Australian Open golf title. He lives in Sydney with wife Sybilla and sons Justin and Roger.

INDEX

NOTES